242514

permanently sensitized

~~TECHNIC BECKETT~~

KU-266-235

LEEDS BECKETT UNIVERSITY
LIBRARY
DISCARDED

Leeds Metropolitan University

TELEPEN

17 0586682 4

STAGE DESIGN

THROUGHOUT THE WORLD

SINCE 1960

INTERNATIONAL THEATRE INSTITUTE PUBLICATIONS

DIRECTOR: RENE HAINAUX

First published in Belgium 1972
(c) Editions Méddens, S.A., Brussels 1972

First published in Great Britain 1973
by GEORGE G. HARRAP & CO. LTD
182-184 High Holborn, London WC1V 7AX

English translation (c) *Editions Meddens, S.A., Brussels* 1973

All rights reserved. No part of this
publication may be reproduced in any
form or by any means without the prior
permission of George G. Harrap & Co. Ltd

ISBN 0 245 51941 6

Printed in Belgium

STAGE DESIGN
throughout the world
since 1960

text and illustrations collected by the national centres of the
international theatre institute
chosen and presented by rené hainaux
with the collaboration of yves-bonnat

foreword by
paul-louis mignon
I.T.I. editorial adviser

HARRAP   LONDON

1705866824

7b 242514

CITY OF LEEDS AND CARNEGIE
COLLEGE LIBRARY

Class 792.025

Acc 73486 V

FOREWORD

Of what remains of the ephemeral adventure of the theatre, the setting possesses pre-eminently the value of a symbol. It bears witness to the communion, in spirit and sensibility, of the playwright and his scene designer.

But the scene designer has worked in agreement with the director, and for the costumes, he has taken the special features of each actor into account. He provides a framework and a structure; the lines of circulation of the characters are made evident in it. It corresponds lastly, by reason of its aesthetics, to the public's possibilities of then accepting its forms.

Thus, when closely examined, it is the dramatic work in performance, in its life as a theatrical organism, and in its relationships with the society of the moment, that we can begin to identify.

This is why the International Theatre Institute took the initiative of bringing out a work on the data and the evolution of contemporary stage design as seen through the personalities of the world's most notable artists. This work appeared in 1954, under the title of *Stage Design throughout the World since 1935*. Twenty-three countries were represented in it.

The interest and the success of the undertaking prompted us to continue it, in 1964, with *Stage Design throughout the World since 1950*. This volume listed the achievements of thirty countries during the 1950-1960 decade. It was supplemented by the valuable « Stage Designers' Who's Who » and the results of an enquiry regarding new techniques and materials.

It thus became evident that the action of the I.T.I. in this field should be followed up regularly in order to allow both stage professionals and theatre-goers to pick up the threads of such a characteristic evolution of the theatre of our century.

The present volume — conceived by those to whom the I.T.I. entrusted full responsibility for the undertaking as long ago as in 1954 : René HAINAUX and YVES-BONNAT (and this time, with the collaboration of Christiane FRAIPONT) — was made the more essential because the theatre itself has been the subject, for the past ten years or so, of arguments that have altered its practices.

To find room, in the limits of a single volume, for the whole of the world's scenographic production was impossible. We considered it more useful to present the developments which, since 1960, and in both the dramatic and musical fields, denote a break with the tradition in the treatment of the classical repertory and of the new forms of drama.

Departing from the conception of the preceding volumes which made use of an alphabetical classification by countries and artists, Christiane FRAIPONT and René HAINAUX have devised a chronological classification by authors, from AESCHYLUS to the young Finnish playwright Henri KAPULAINEN, from MONTEVERDI to the young Dutch composer Peter SCHAT. In bringing together these diverse forms of experience, they have endeavoured to bring out the original contribution of each of them by collecting the scene designers' working-notes.

YVES-BONNAT stresses the analogies and contrasts of techniques or styles; in this way he contributes to a better understanding of the problems of present-day drama and of the ways in which they can be solved.

Thanks to these different propositions, stage design becomes, above all, a guide to dramatic literature and to the lyrical and choreographic repertory, as revealed to us in the most recent productions.

We thank all those — I.T.I. Centres and National Sections of the International Organization of Scenographers and Theatre Technicians, without forgetting various helpful and reliable correspondents — whose collaboration has enabled us to bring this work to a successful conclusion.

PAUL-LOUIS MIGNON

ACKNOWLEDGMENTS

It is not easy to measure the sum of the efforts put up by the National Centres of the International Theatre Institute, or even by our ordinary correspondents, for the compilation of this work.

They have invited the collaboration of scene designers, photographers and collectors, whom we can only thank collectively. They also assumed full responsability for the delicate problem of copyright, of which the solution had necessarily to be regarded as an essential preliminary.

We wish to express our particular gratitude to Mrs Leila Gaad of the Centre for the Arabic Republic of Egypt, to Mr Robert Quentin of the Australian Centre, to the Austrian Institut für Theaterwissenschaft, to Messrs Raymond Renard and Alfons Van Impe of Belgium, to Mr Agostinho Olavo Rodrigues of the Brazilian Centre and to Mrs Olga Obry, to Miss Yolande Bird and Miss Pamela Howard of the British Centre, to Miss Nelly Fillod and Messrs Gilles Rochette and Jack Gray of the Canadian Centre, to Mrs Eva Soukupova of the Czechoslovak Centre, to Mr Max Wagener of the Dutch Centre, to Mr Tuomo Tirkkonen of the Finnish Centre, to Messrs Yves-Bonnat and Paul-Louis Mignon of the French Centre, to Mr Friedrich Dieckmann of the Centre for the German Democratic Republic and of the OISTT, to Mrs Gerda Dietrich of the Centre for the Federal Republic of Germany, to Mrs Suzanne Gal of the Hungarian Centre, to Mr Gudlaugur Rosinkranz of the Icelandic Centre, to Mrs Margalit Sela and Mr Jesaja Weinberg of the Israeli Centre, to Mr Noël Vaz of Jamaica, to Mr Tomoo Tobari of the Japanese Centre as well as to Mr Akira Wakabayashi, to the Kanamori Corporation and to Mr Shizuko Sato Katatani, to Messrs Wole Soyinka and J.A. Adedeji of Nigeria, to Mrs Eva Roïne of the Norwegian Centre, to Mr Lamberto V. Avellana of the Centre for the Philippines, to Mr Zygmunt Hübner of the Polish Centre, to Mrs Margareta Barbutza of the Rumanian Centre, to Mr Maurice Sonar Senghor of the Senegalese Centre, to Mr Carmelo Romero of the Spanish Centre, to Mrs Ingrid Luterkort of the Swedish Centre, to Mr Edmond Stadler of the Swiss Centre, to Mrs Elizabeth Burdick of the U.S.A. Centre and to Mr Joël Rubin of the OISTT, to Mr Vassili Goussev of the U.S.S.R. Centre, to Mr Humberto Orsini of the Venezuelan Centre, to Messrs Mladja Veselinovic and Miomir Denic of the Yugoslav Centre.

We should also like to mention the invaluable help afforded by Mr Ossia Trilling, Vice-President of the International Association of Theatre Critics, in agreeing to revise the English translation of Mr Yves-Bonnat's article, as well as the unfailing encouragement given by Mr Jean Darcante, Secretary General of the I.T.I., to our work.

Lastly, we must acknowledge our indebtedness to the Prague Quadrennial of Theatre Design and Architecture. The admirable exhibitions put on by the latter in Prague in 1967, and then in 1971, have greatly increased our knowledge, excited our imagination and facilitated our work.

THE THEATRE REAPPRAISED

"Construction cumbers the ground with institutions made by busybodies.
Destruction clears it and gives us breathing space and liberty. ... You confuse
construction and destruction with creation and murder."

(George Bernard SHAW — 1901)

This book is not an accumulation, but a choice or, in other words, a necessarily biased selection. Our purpose is to bear witness to the theatre of the sixties : given our inability to draw up a complete and objective balance-sheet for the years in question—an of course superhuman task—we have endeavoured to bring out the most original aspects of the said decade.

In agreement with the International Theatre Institute, this third volume of "Stage Design throughout the World" is thus devoted essentially to the non-traditional aspects of the performing arts.

The first circular letters addressed to the I.T.I. Centres and to our correspondents reflected this intention. Way back in January 1970 we wrote :

"By concentrating on non-traditional productions, we wish to bring out, in our book, the changes that have occured in the conception of stage design—its role, its aesthetic aspect, its materialization—during the past ten years. These changes are the outcome of a number of factors which have operated now separately, now simultaneously :

1° the search for a new place of performance

2° the development of a political ideology as opposed to art for art's sake

3° the experiments of the laboratory theatre, which—however varied they may be—often have in common the yearning for a certain 'sacred theatre'."

When we decided on this line of action, we realized that the results would not be homogeneous. Internationalization has undoubtedly promoted exchanges, but the face of the theatre is not yet the same in London and Moscow, in Caracas and Stockholm. And the terms "traditional" and "non-traditional" still admit, depending on the countries, of dissimilar acceptances.

We have not always had the heart to rule out a specific example of living tradition in which director and scenographer have made a point of recapturing the original intention of the author or the composer. But, on the whole, our selection has opted for productions for which director and scenographer have agreed on a conception of the theatre or on a "reading" of the work that would have been unthinkable before 1960.

Many innovators of the sixties make no bones about stating : "This work interests me not by reason of what it may have had to say, but by reason of what it allows me to say today". Such remarks inspire terror and often call down anathema, ... generally on the part of older section of the directors, the public and the critics.

But the rising generation appreciates the efforts of those who keep up—somewhat belatedly, for that matter—with the torrential evolution of the sciences, literature and the arts. In the coming years, what theatre artist will still dare to ignore the attainments of psycho-analysis and of sociology ? Strehler handles Brechtian dialectics with complete success, Jung and Moreno have no further secrets for Grotowski.

The use of new methods of analysis and their application by men of talent to works of which the message seemed definitely fixed lead to the discovery of unexpected aspects of the said works. In this period of change, successes are rare and the models hard to detect. The first tangible result is to render totally unacceptable what was up till yesterday regarded as satisfactory. This is illustrated in a particularly striking manner by the case of Racine in France : during the first half of the present century, no stage professional remodelled the presentation of his tragedies to a notable extent ; nowadays, it has become almost impossible for a director to tackle Racine without taking the contributions of Mauron, Goldmann and Barthes into account.

Does this mean that a bridge has at last been established between academic research and stage practice ? This cannot be affirmed without presumption. But that frail structures have been cast across is beyond doubt. And every one knows that a wonderful *King Lear* was born of a meeting—Picaresque in some regards—between director Peter Brook and professor Jan Kott.

The presentation chosen for this volume brings us, in the first place, a survey of the classics from Aeschylus to Schiller, by way of Shakespeare.

Then comes what is commonly called the modern theatre. Brecht—and this is no surprise— has been played extensively during the past ten years ; less expected is the place occupied by such playwrights as Witkiewicz, Genet, Weiss or Arrabal.

Here, too, our choice is questionable. To begin with, it is composite : we had at heart to retain productions which were "non-traditional" from the angle of dramatic conception and from that of scenographic achievement. And the two do not always go together.

For Yves-Bonnat, the history of the past ten years is that of an evolution ; what he stresses in his panoramic contribution are the filiations. We, on the other hand, are struck by the reappraisal involved, by the ruptures.

A question of perspective rather than of actual facts ?

We are perhaps over sensitive to the contradictions of our societies and of our civilization ? We may tend to exaggerate the role of the contestatory fraction amongst our theatre people ? We perhaps attach too much importance to the mechanism which leads on from participation to provocation ?

The reader will at least admit that we are not alone in reacting in this manner.

Ample proof of this claim is afforded by the comparison which we borrow from the French daily "Le Monde" (October 21, 1971). It opposes, in two columns, the theory of the popular theatre as defined, notably, by Vilar and the French Dramatic Centres in 1950, and that of 1970 as it can be deduced from the declarations of some young animators.

Although not a universally applicable schema, this table has been reproduced and commented on in the international press and has elicited varying reactions from theatre people in many countries.

Shall we at least admit that the questions asked go to the heart of the problem ? And that they most obviously entail important repercussions in the fields of scenography ?

René HAINAUX - Christiane FRAIPONT

Two Theories

of popular theatre

In the fifties	In the seventies
WHERE	
New premises	The street, the place of work
Without proscenium arch	Without any fixed structure
Towards the public	Amidst the public
FOR WHOM	
The greatest number	Small groups
To draw the public	To go out to the public
All classes intermingled	The working classes first
To educate the spectator	To defer to the spectator
To promote the demand for season-tickets	To promote on-the-spot adhesion
BY WHOM	
Artists assisting the public	Artists serving the public
Legitimate heirs	Voluntary bastards
Craftsmen	Amateurs
Specialists of the expression	Spontaneous militants
Directors	Agitators
FOR WHAT PURPOSE	
Culture for all	A political battle
Cultural democracy	Permanent revolution
Better order	Disorder
HOW	
Good theatre per se	Theatre per se does not exist
Up with the classics	Down with the classics
To clean up the heritage	To refuse any kind of heritage
To exalt what unites	To show what must divide
To seek for the universal	To denounce the class contents
Lyrical illusion	Lesson in realism
To reconcile the hero and the world	To invite to battle
To change the work-stage relationship	To change the stage-public relationship
Passive admiration	Active participation
Cult of the hero	Exaltation of the group
Rite	Festival
Moral education	Physical explosion
Rigour	Exuberance
Necessary Utopia	Possible victory
Generous theory	Violent practice
Applause	Slogans
Reflection	Action

(From "Le Monde", October 21, 1971)

DÉCOR : NO

SCENE DESIGN : YES

by YVES-BONNAT

A serious study of recent developments in contemporary scene design cannot be divorced from that of the theatrical activity of which it is a part, though there is still no way of telling which entails the other, even when a great many experts, rightly or wrongly, still proclaim the primacy of the director.

The interaction between the changes that have occurred in scene design—settings, costumes, and lighting—and those affecting the place of performance, which might conveniently be termed "spatial scenographic structures", is just as hard to determine. On the one hand, the links between stage and auditorium in a traditional picture-frame type of theatre have been modified. Elsewhere, the absence of a playhouse has been overcome by improvising some sort of workable framework in makeshift premises: in a circus tent, a gymnasium, a shed, and so on. Elsewhere again, because of aesthetic preference or of an uncertain future which argues caution, the decision to build any kind of framework whatever has been deliberately avoided. A final example applies to the type of scene design that has been made to house a particular work and this has automatically conditioned its shape. And, in a very general way, when it comes to constructing something quite new, directors, producers, and scene designers either have to fight the lack of competence and the conservatism of the authorities, or else they forget that a very small number of architects throughout the world are specialists and have broken fresh ground in the field of "spatial scenographic structures".

*

The picture-frame type of theatre was of course perfect for the needs of the aristocracy and the middle-classes throughout the past two centuries. It imposed a form of scene design based on perspective and illusion, and each contrived to create a reality of a kind. It did not prevent attempts at modernization: "naturalism", which substituted true for false appearances; "aestheticism", which introduced a magnified painter's easel-piece on this stage; or "constructivism", which was born of the union of light and volume. But it has perpetuated the segregation of actor and spectator. And it is precisely against this segregation that theatre people today wish to fight by approaching the notion of space from an entirely new angle.

MULTI-PURPOSE AND FLEXIBLE STAGING

They are looking for a new theatre, which the Berlin scene designer Andreas REINHARDT has tried to define as follows :

> "A variable theatre in every sense. Above all, in the relationship between stage and audience: and with any number of variants between the two extremes of the optical box-set and the arena-type stage surrounded on all sides by the audience. The proscenium arch would be variable, flies would be fitted in the auditorium. The whole theatre would look like a workshop rather than a festive hall. The full flexibility of the resultant structure would correspond to the fact that in modern drama (no less than in the theatres' repertoire) there is neither a compulsory style, nor a single technical method that demands an unequivocal theatrical space."(1)

It is worth linking to this search the scientific analysis of the notion of space in the theatre that the French architect and scene designer Jacques BOSSON attempts to define:

> "Dramatic space must be subordinated to metric truth. Quarter-tones are used in music, shades of meaning in psychology, and micro-decisions in town-planning: these concepts of the bearing one interval may have on another have their counterpart in the composition of dramatic space. This space must be a container that can both acquire and lay down different dramatic gradations that have previously been graduated by the person who is building the outer framework. This will often, and before anything else can be undertaken, mean a space-time of which the dimensions are going to be determined by the length of the spectator's stay and this in turn will entail constantly changing focal points of various kinds that will depend on the different positions he and his fellow spectators occupy in the layout. This way we arrive at a diaphragm-space or, if you prefer, an accordion-space."

Theatre-architects and scene designers attending international seminaries and colloquies during the past decade have agreed unanimously on the need to modify the "spatial structure" of the production. The adjectives most commonly used in discussion—"experimental", "multi-purpose", "modular", "flexible", "mobile", "transportable", "collapsible" and even "inflatable"—are significant of the identity of views to be found today. These are similar to the wish once expressed by Adolphe APPIA: *"Let us abandon these theatres to their moribund past, let us erect simple buildings that are merely intended to provide a roof for the space we work in —no stage, no auditorium, simply a bare and empty room."*

There are some designers who have managed to move on from theory to practice, like the architect Jean DARRAS and the scene designer Bernard GUILLAUMOT who built the "Théâtre des Amandiers" in Nanterre (in France) in 1969. Quick changes of the inside allow this deliberately homogeneously shaped free volume to be used to stage productions "in the ancient manner" (i.e. frontally), on the "apron stage" (i.e. Elizabethan-style), "in the round" or "on simultaneous stages".

THE MEANS OF COMMUNICATION

A large number of examples of this type of theatre building can be found all over the world. Their volume and style may differ but they reflect the same trend: "trend" rather than "actual realization" because the process is continuous, as for instance in the case of the "Simulation Laboratory" founded by a Pedagogic Unit of the "Ecole des Beaux-Arts" in Paris or, again, when certain productions are fitted into so-called "free" spaces. This applies to the American-inspired "happening", to the French director Ariane MNOUCHKINE's *1789* and *1793,* to the Italian Luca RONCONI's *Orlando Furioso*, and so on. This trend also leads to the concept of "integrated theatre", to which the Swiss couple, Pierre and Anne-Marie SIMOND, have devoted a particularly detailed study:

> "PROPOSITION. The theatre is a place for information and for human intercourse. If it is linked to other activities of the same kind, it becomes a mere incident in a walk through the town: the attractions of the High-Street, the presence of shops and restaurants, and the nearby bus-station will facilitate the living integration of the performing arts into urban life. Whether occasional or daily, an encounter with the play and its production can only make the theatre more familiar. In the same way, the integration of theatrical premises into other centres of activity increases the available number of the inhabitants who are the ultimate consumers. Going to the theatre virtually becomes a daily habit.
> (. . .)
>
> THE INTEGRATED THEATRE. The advantage of the convention of the street-theatre is that it addresses the passer-by directly. But by the very reason of its limited technical means it excludes a great many forms of expression. An INTEGRATED THEATRE, on the other hand, by opening on to the street and, consequently, on to daily life, offers theatrical premises that are both technically highly developed and flexible, because freed from the constraints of the traditional theatre.
> (. . .)
>
> As opposed to a multi-purpose auditorium, the INTEGRATED THEATRE lends itself to the creation of specific spaces. It also makes possible a number of assemblages based on standardized components." (3)

Innovations should be tackled with caution, for, as will be seen, if the desire for "communication" constitutes the major concern of most architects, directors and stage designers, the means of attaining it differ appreciably. In this connection, an example of one of the most highly effective could be that adopted by Luca RONCONI for his *Orlando Furioso* (see illustrations n° 43-45). It is described by the theatrical authority Ettore CAPRIOLO as follows:

> "... here, there is absolutely no distinction between the spectator's area and the actor's: the two areas intermingle, overlap, and penetrate each other. The different stage actions can develop at any point whatever of the rectangle, and often, as has been stated, at several points at once. The actors enter, as a rule, on trucks pushed from beneath, from behind or from side by other players not being used for the time being, and they have to force their way through the spectators. These trucks are bare and carry either actors on their own or polished tin horses constructed somewhat after the manner of Sicilian puppets, a resemblance that is certainly not accidental. The fact is that these are stage machines that look what they are, stage props with no more or less naturalistic element of make-believe added to them: they have the elemental power of suggestion and arouse in the spectator an innocent wonder like that of his lost childhood." (4)

Jerzy GROTOWSKI, with his Laboratory Theatre, attempts not only to bring the spectator closer to the performance but actually to implicate him. He will have no such thing as a privileged spectator in the auditorium. The spectators' seats appear to have been placed here and there at random; in fact, they are put in position according to very precise plans, that oblige the actors to move about betwen them in a manner that enhances their power to act on, and not simply before, these spectators.

Unlike *Orlando Furioso* and *1789,* whose action unfolds among large crowds, GROTOWSKI's productions involve a small number of people: it is a theatre for the happy few, conceived in a perspective at total variance with that of the "happening", which created a scandal in its early days but now appears to be a thing of the past. One cannot say that these experiments and theories are without interest. But what does the audience think of all these many-angled productions presented to them by their no less generous producers? Where can these productions be put on?

Can they take the place of the complex traditional theatre? Are they suited to all types of drama? Can one accept the co-existence of several forms of theatrical production? Can the written work maintain its primacy in the total dramaturgic act? Are strictly new formulas likely to be accepted spontaneously in every country and by every generation? All these questions will receive divergent answers. Some will be motivated by a conservative outlook, others by a rejection of tradition (of content and form), or by a pressing desire to return to the fountain-head. Faced with this dilemma, the Polish critic, Jerzy KOENIG, voices certain fears:

> "A theatre which would change its character every twenty-five years, and in which the new generation would try to start everything from the beginning, wiping out everything its predecessors had done, would be of little interest, to be sure. This would mean that this art does not know how to create durable values, that it changes in furious waves, scorning tradition, cultural continuity, durability of institutions and homogeneity of style. This would mean that every twenty-five years a new "Comédie Française" would arise, a new "Burgtheater", a new "Moscow Art Theatre", burying the achievements, output and fame of its predecessors. This would also mean that the form of contemporary art would have to be determined by individual action, by the young talents of an élite group of producers for whose activity nothing—not the social life, the political structure of the country, the layout of social forces, the interests of the audience nor the achievements in other fields of art—was of any great importance." (5)

The American, Harold CLURMAN, sounds a more confident, and even more optimistic, note:

> "Everywhere—in community centers, universities, libraries, churches, cafés, cellars, dining places, lofts, literally in the streets and fields—theatrical groups are being formed. Despite films, radio and television, the appetite for living theatre has not entirely waned. It may be once again in the ascendant.

> Of what value is this new or renewed development? The question answers itself. Such activity—even when failure accompanies the various projects—is always healthy. For a flower to grow, the seed must first decay. Theatre flourishes on a subsoil of organic matter. Much effort which momentarily appears wasted precedes the birth of new life". (6)

The lessons that can be drawn from the new situation of the theatre are disquieting in so far as the aesthetic concepts are the product of all the socio-cultural reappraisals. Whatever the type of theatre concerned—"experimental", "laboratory", "research" or even "avant-garde"—the common anxiety is to express and to spread a modern form of thought for the benefit of a putative audience—in other words, an audience that has still to be won over—by the most efficacious means, even if they seem at first sight unusual, and by a mostly collective type of organization not directly concerned with making a profit.

THE SCENE DESIGNER IN THE CREATIVE GROUP

What place then does the scene designer occupy in this organization? It would seem that the principles of artistic choice that once decided his designation by the manager and by the director have been more or less generally replaced by an authentic meeting of minds between these two—or the "producer", who often combines the two roles—and the scene designer, and by his actual incorporation into the team of technicians and players.

Before inquiring into the working methods of some of the best scene designers of today, a look at the stages each must go through, and the difficulties he has to meet, would be helpful.

The scene designer must, of course, begin by acquainting himself with the dramatic work: the written play or the scenario for an improvised show. This entails a full-scale dialectical analysis, accompanied by research into the philosophical, historical or political references, and this will of course lead to his accepting the spirit of the projected production. His compliance having being obtained, there follows the stage of the discussions with the director, of the weight given to his conception and of the personal contributions that will lead to its visual and dynamic realisation. When the company is a "group", the discussions are widened to include questions of acting and technical presentation. In our view, this is the best way, because enriching to all alike, and naturally exhilarating. But because the traditionally approved division into compartments is so hard to kill and perhaps also because the daily work of the painter is an individual act with a possibly different social purpose, this way is still unfortunately rare. This explains the progressive replacement of painters in stage matters by plastic artists skilled in different media, and by architects. On the other hand, the scene designer, so long confined to his role of creator of works of art and unwilling to soil his hands, has today begun to invent new staging processes and to work side by side with the technician-workman—the carpenter, the smith, the mechanic, the scene painter, the modeller—as well as with the dressmaker, the electrician or the sound-technician. This collaboration excites his imagination and multiplies his means of expression. Being present at rehearsals helps him to understand the actors' special problems and suggest fresh solutions.

This is the path things have taken in recent times. They have turned out to be so generally accepted that they have led, in certain of our cultural centres, "Maisons de Culture", and universities, to the formation of teams of scene designers—cum—creative-producers, and to the introduction of teaching methods in performing arts schools.

The definition of the French term "scénographe", one that seems to impose itself internationally in preference to those used until now, i.e.: "décorateur" (French), "scene designer" (English), "Bühnenbildner" (German), "decoratore"

(Italian), "décorontwerper" (Dutch), "dekorator" (Swedish), is given by Chamfort, the XVIIIth-century French moralist: *"A man experienced in drawing, painting, sculpture, architecture and perspective who invents and executes or sets out painted works of architecture and all sorts of decoration necessary to the theatre"*.

It will be seen that this definition does not conflict with the spoken or written ideas of contemporary scene designers. The Frenchman, Jacques NOËL, for example, writes:

"In the present situation of the theatre, being a scene designer is to select—therefore to invent—in a repertoire of which painters and sculptors explore the resources, those which correspond to what an author (dramatist, poet or musician) postulates in order that his work may attain its fullest efficacy. This supposes, on the part of the scene designer, a technique, a craftsmanship totally different from that of the painter or sculptor, with whom he is often confused because of the means employed—although the fact that these means are deployed in a manner far closer to that of the author is too often overlooked." (7)

The Czech, Josef SVOBODA, writes:

"A plastic language.
In the modern theatre, stage design together with the other elements used, has the function of communicating to the audience an artistic reality in which all the parts work in harmony.

Fundamentally, it is not a question of the accidental composition of elements or even relationships, but the creation of dramatic plans which can be changed in the course of the action, appearing and disappearing as required by the dramatic tension. Modern "scenography" cannot borrow the means of expression from other branches of art but must create its own plastic language." (8)

Add to this statement that of the Czech director, Otomar KREJCA, with whom Josef SVOBODA has collaborated on several productions:

"The best stage design...

"Scenography" as such is a virtually incommunicable art once it is separated from the production as a whole. It is intransmissible if the designer is what he should be, that is to say one of the contributors to a certain dramatic style. Sketches or models of designs are but poor copies of what the latter were on the stage. No exhibition of stage design can compare with the veritable revue of dramatic art which unfolds every evening before the spectators of the world's theatres.

The stage design that has no independent meaning is the best." (7)

It should be noted that the foregoing are the opinions of professionals who have worked mainly in old theatres and who, having no "multi-purpose" or flexible auditoriums at their disposal, have—without demolishing the walls—attempted to break apart the proscenium arch of the picture-frame type of stage by means of ingenious "scenographic" arrangements and an intelligent use of lighting, within the optical boundaries of the acting area. In this connection the Frenchman, René ALLIO, who was involved in the re-designing and re-building of the "Théâtre Sarah Bernhardt" in Paris as the "Théâtre de la Ville", adopts a liberal attitude:

"Use of space...

More than the form of the stage and the theatre, it is the way in which one makes use of this space (from the point of view of stage design as well as production and acting) that will determine whether the nature of the performance given will be one of illusion or not, one of participation or of alienation. The problem of theatre architecture as it is generally raised today is thus seen in its true light: it is a false problem. "Alienated" theatre is possible on a picture-frame type of stage, and make-believe theatre on an apron stage." (8)

This same liberalism marks the work of many scene designers. Take the case of the Swede, Carl-Johan STRÖM, who modestly declares:

"My theatrical colleagues and I always say that starting work on a new production ought to be the same thing as embarking on a new profession. Methods, materials and technique should be strictly adapted to the character of the enterprise." (7)

THE DECORATION AND THE DECORATIVE

The East-German Andreas REINHARDT quoted above, goes even further in stating: *"I find that there is no prescription for creating a stage design"*. This remarks serves as an introduction to the declarations of his compatriot Karl von APPEN, who has studied the problem in detail from the twofold angle of Brechtian working methods and the organization of the theatre in the German Democratic Republic:

"The Decoration and the Decorative.

It is particularly difficult to define the work of the stage designer. In German, the word "Dekoration" is used as well as "Ausstattung"—both terms recall in a negative sense the "decorator" and the "outfitter"—and most people speak of "Bühnenbild" (literally "stage picture"), but in reality the stage is—even if perceived in the way pictures are—a space and must be dealt with as such. The meaning of the term "Bühnenbildner" ("stage designer")—can only be fully appreciated if the sense of the verb it is derived from is realised: "bilden" ("to design", in the sense of "to form", "to create", "to shape"); that is, the stage designer is not somebody who makes stage pictures ("Bühnenbildner"), but someone who "designs" the stage ("die Bühne bilden"). In this sense too, both the author and the director are also "stage shapers".

The word "Dekoration" ("scenery") has long since become a technical term—a collective term for everything on the stage apart from the actors. But the other meaning of the word "Dekoration"—i.e. "dressing up", "adorning oneself"—constitutes a latent danger for the work of the stage designer.

I would define the decorative design of a stage as that kind of scenery that makes the static elements of the scene independent of the dynamic ones, i.e. independent of the actions of the actors, whether they "act" one beside the other, or even whether the stage design, the scenic exterior, dominates the action on the stage. (...) Such a conception of design will almost always impress and win the applause of the audience if it is splendidly done. But the audience—applauding decorative scenery of this kind when the curtain rises—will, in due course, be unable to resist a kind of creeping embarrassment and, even if unconsciously, will allow the attention to stray between the setting and the action on the stage.

Every production is a very sensitive system of equilibrium, a balancing act of many individual kinds of art involved, of the "sister arts" as Brecht used to say—the production is an adjustment, a bringing into focus of its weights and possibilities, a process of integration which, by adding the individual factors, brings forth a new artistic quality —in short the theatre itself—and which can only be successful if it succeeds in achieving this conversion of the sum into the total." (1)

The conclusion is drawn by REINHARDT, who quotes von APPEN:

"The only established principle in our work is the dialectical approach, which does not say: this or that, but: this and that at the same time, not to "cover up", but to "uncover"." (1)

The Frenchman, Michel RAFAËLLI, who shares this opinion, writes about his scene designs for *Medea,* a work first staged at the 1967 Avignon Festival in France:

"Every production raises a totality of problems to be solved. Among them is that of the use of materials. Since this is often linked to financial considerations, their choice is extremely limited for that very reason. This perhaps explains why the theatre has lagged behind other artistic disciplines and the general run of contemporary industrial techniques. But financial constraints do not excuse everything. Lack of curiosity and interest in the innumerable discoveries that exist today can also be cited.

The only way of opening up the theatre to the contemporary world might be precisely to turn it into a pulpit, a meeting-place for the most varied disciplines, where every stage of the work in hand would be entrusted to artists who, in the last resort, alone are capable of transforming its means." (9)

Lastly, here are some concrete examples of the work of a modern scene designer as given by the Frenchman, André ACQUART:

"In my work, I let myself be guided above all by intuition. I try to imagine the acting of all the players, all their movements. I create a setting which is intended to be an ideal acting machine, a sculpture of the scenic space, and I try to bring the setting to life... The desire to create a walkway for the players to act on is a constant in my work."

To analyse the play, to serve it, to serve the director, to serve the actors, and to win the support of the public, these are the scene designer's main objects, whatever his school or country.

This said, let us examine the aesthetic and technical forms which offer an outlet for the expression of personalities of today's scene designer.

INTERDEPENDENCE OF TECHNIQUE AND AESTHETICS

The aesthetic forms of present-day scene design continue to be closely linked to those of the plastic arts, from the new figurative to the abstract, by way of surrealism, Op art, pop art, psychedelic art, advertising, draughtsmanship, kineticism, commercial design, functional architecture and documentary or stylistic photography. The links between them consist of reciprocal borrowings and influences, and these explain the speed with which innovations come about. Gone is the time when painted canvas hung or nailed on wooden frames delimited the formal field of vision of the scene-painter. Modern scenery is "really" spatial. It can thus link up with sculpture and architecture, and be composed either of authentically noble materials (metal, wood, leather, etc.), or of synthetic ones of multiple appearance and use. It is no longer built in a representational manner but in an expressionist one, by the selection of dominant components. Electrical techniques favour and even tend to develop this selective conception either by focussing attention on a given place (which can also be one of the actors), or by complementing the setting by means of limited lighting, by the total or partial projection of graphic, photographic or cinematographic documents. The most recent technique to be employed is that of laser beams: thanks to their combination, veritable dancing light-patterns can be projected without the use of a screen.

Even stage-machinery has been vastly improved thanks to new appartus, often invented by various scene designers who, like RAFFAËLLI, call themselves "mechanics".

As a result, costumes too have to undergo similar changes: the materials chosen should be suggestive and suitable for "catching the light", their cut suggestive rather than realistic. These choices can lead to the costume being regarded as complementary to the setting and, in some cases, as the setting itself. Some of the best results can be obtained by means of the mask: the make-up mask, the costume-mask, the puppet-mask, or the costume-décor-mask. And it is here where the connection with the antique Greek theatre or, more precisely, with the primitive African theatre, can be seen.

Faced with this wealth of means, it is hard to find the exact words in which to describe the aesthetic trends of those who know how to use them. Let us borrow some of the terms proposed by our Polish colleague Zenobiusz STRZELECKI:

"To Karl von APPEN's "scenography" (Berliner Ensemble), I would give the name of synthetic naturalism, while Polish "scenography" is dominated by a "supranaturalism", with symbolic tendencies (Jozef SZAJNA, Wojciech KRAKOWSKI...). In France, René ALLIO's scene designs are more analytical, more intellectual; Michel RAFFAËLLI is more attracted by primitive workmanship, by simple and dynamic forms. In Czechoslovakia, the settings of Ladislav VYCHODIL, Vladimir SUCHANEK, Vladimir SRAMEK and Stefan HUDAK present a distinctly neo-naturalist character. In the U.S.S.R., scene design takes on a less extreme character and the tendencies represented by the late Anatoli BOSSULAIEV and Nisson SHIFRIN, and by Nikolaj ZOLOTAREV might be defined by the term "expressive realism"; more nimble workmanship and a more synthetic approach characterize the scene designers of the Taganka Theatre (Enar STENBERG and David BOROVSKIJ).

In the kinetic works of the Czech, Josef SVOBODA, I see examples which are akin to Op art by reason of the abstract character of the form used, of the "twinkling" produced by movement or by the recourse to a multiplicity of mirrors, as well as by the black-and-white colouring.

A relatively general tendency is towards neo-constructivism, in which the practically abstract skeleton, of wood or metal, is decked out with more naturalistic elements. This skeleton is perforated, functional and sometimes kinetic. It contains stage-properties and architectural fragments treated with total realism."

STRZELECKI concludes his study by pointing out, as we have done, that:

"There are theatres which reject all settings, whatever their nature, and above all the picture-frame type of stage, which leads, by its very nature, to the "peep-show" image and, by consequence, to placing the spectator outside the action. In these theatres, the "scenography" is above all an architectural feature of the auditorium: Shakespeare and the Elizabethan stage remain its model."

Lastly, STRZELECKI recalls the elimination, by GROTOWSKI, of the permanent box-set; the task of his scene designer, Jerzy GURAWSKI, is to set out the space occupied by the spectators and the actors in terms of their mutual roles: communion, observation and isolation. But in these productions too, STRZELECKI admits the presence of neo-naturalist elements: the fences are made of real wood, the beds of iron, the stove-pipes of metal sheeting...

One can say that the setting in these productions, as in those of the "Living Theatre" and of "Odin Teatret", is marginal.

A THEATRE OF TOTALITY

But there exists a word which has not as yet been employed in this text: namely "magic". Apart from the traditional theatre and from the documentary theatre, numerous productions—some at the research stage, some finished products—have shown us that magic intervenes more and more frequently on the stage. This reveals a more or less conscious, but apparently sincere, desire to "return to the sources". Does it indicate a trend towards the resurgence of the "total theatre", that Jean-Louis BARRAULT proposes to call "theatre of totality"? We have inherited the successes, the experience and the theories of the dramatists, directors and scene designers who preceded us. We have at our disposal technical processes and equipment which are being modernised all the time. We can thus bring together, in a single production, dramatic art, lyric art, choreographic art, pantomime and the arts of the circus and of the music-hall... use new materials and the infinite combinations of electric energy: from lighting to the audio-visual, by way of electro-mechanism. But certain architectural problems posed by the musical theatre with a live orchestra have still to be solved. In this connection, let us quote the words of the East-German scene designer Reinhart ZIMMERMANN:

"I do not think that opera is more dependent than are other genres on the proscenium-stage. It is true that the architecture of the majority of theatres forces the stage designer to tackle this problem. There are two ways of solving it. The peep-show optics can be stressed by framing the setting; this creates a certain distance between the audience and the stage which may very well promote the understanding of the problems of the past. One can also try to overcome the peep-show optics, for instance, by including architectural elements of the auditorium into the stage design. Such a purely decorative break-through in the structure can, of course, only be useful if the stage is really extended in the direction of the audience, e.g. by partially building over the orchestra pit". (1)

ZIMMERMANN then defines the role of the scene designer in the musical theatre:

"The operatic stage is a field of musical action (...). The music determines the dimensions of the field of action. The interrelationship between the optical and the acoustical is quite considerable... Even the degree of light makes an impact on the hearing of the music. It is this aspect which basically distinguishes the performance of an opera from a record or a concert." (1)

The opinion of the Soviet scene designer, Valerij L

> "The stage designer must express the then
> the music, the passages from one theme
> the next."

The promoters of the "theatre of totality" owe it to
insert non-recorded musical passages into their producti
to architects and scene designers.

But if the "theatre of totality" is to succeed, other
which must govern the transformations of our society.
graphers" in particular—should be awake to all the
world, and, we very much hope, enrich them through t

SOURCES :

(1) *Bühnenbildarbeit in der Deutschen Demokratischen Republik.*
Mit Texten von Karl von Appen, Heinrich Kilger, Andreas
Sowie 57 Abbildungen von dem DDR-Beitrag zur Prager Q
Herausgegeben von der Sektion DDR der Internationalen O
Stage Design in the German Democratic Republic.
Texts by Karl von Appen, Heinrich Kilger, Andreas Reinh
With 57 illustrations from the GDR contribution to the Se
Published by the GDR Section of the International Organisa

(2) See, in particular : Les Lieux du Spectacle, special issue of
(France).

(3) " Le Théâtre intégré " by Pierre Simond and Anne-Marie Sin

(4) " *Le Roland Furieux* sur la place publique " by Ettore Capr

(5) " New Producers " by Jerzy Koenig in The Theatre in Po

(6) " Je sème partout " by Harold Clurman in *American The*
York 1969.

(7) " Quinze ans de décoration théâtrale française " in L'Inform

(8) *Stage Design Throughout the World since 1950.* Internatio
London, 1964.

(9) " Péripéties d'une recherche technique " by Michel Raffaëlli i

KEY TO THE CAPTIONS
UNDER THE
ILLUSTRATIONS

A. DRAMA (ill. 1 to 416) and
GROUPS (ill. 417 to 427)

First, the name of the playwright, the date
of birth and possibly the date of death, the
name of the adapter if the latter has altered
the play to a notable extent.

Next, the title of the work in its original
language.

1. Name of the designer.
2. Name of the director.
3. Name of the composer.
4. Name of the choreographer.
5. Name of the company and/or of the theatre,
   followed by the town and the year of production.
6. Name of the photographer.

B. OPERA — BALLET — MUSICAL
(ill. 428 to 534)

First, the name of the composer, the date of
birth and possibly the date of death.

Next, the title of the work in its original
language.

1. Name of the designer.
2. Name of the director.
3. Name of the librettist or of the author
   whose work has been used for the libretto.
4. Name of the choreographer.
5. Name of the company and/or of the theatre,
   followed by the town and the year of production.
6. Name of the photographer.

* This asterisk, following some captions, refers to explanations given on pages 223 to 226.

ARRANGEMENT
OF ILLUSTRATIONS

The illustrations are classified in the chronological order of the playwrights for drama (pp 17 to 168) and of the composers for the musical theatre (pp 175 to 216). Pages 169 to 174 are devoted to the "GROUPS" whose productions are collective undertakings without it being possible to attribute the "play" to an "author".

The captions accompanying the illustrations have been drafted in keeping with a code which makes them international.

In the first place, the title of the work is given in its original language. For instance, for Gorki's The Lower Depths, *presented in Prague, we have adopted the original Russian title,* Na Dne, *rather than its translation into Czech. And in line with the same principle, José Triana's* The Assassins, *presented in Holland, figures under its original title of* La Noche de los Asesinos.

The English translation of these original titles can be found in the indexes.

We have dispensed with the name of the country when the town concerned is the capital : Caracas, Helsinki, Tokio ... When the town is not the capital, the name of the country follows between brackets ; this name may prove somewhat surprising : Hungary is styled "Magyarorszag", Norway "Norge", the German Democratic Republic "D.D.R." (Deutsche Demokratische Republik), the Federal Republic of Germany "B.R.D." Bundesrepublik Deutschland), Switzerland "Helvetia" ...

1. – AISCHYLOS (525-456): *Oresteia*. **1**: Franco Nonnis.
2: Antonio Calenda. **3**: Domenico Guaccero. **5**: Teatro
Stabile dell'Aquila. Aquila (Italia). 1970.
6: Cesidio Gualtieri. *

2. – AISCHYLOS (525-456): *Persai*. **1**: Wim Vesseur. **2**: Erik Vos. **3**: Rudolf Escher. **4**: Erik Vos. **5**: De Nieuwe Komedie en het Holland Festival. Carré. Amsterdam (Nederland). 1963. **6**: Maria Austria – Henk Jonker.

3. – AISCHYLOS (525-456) – HUBERT GIGNOUX: *La Prise de l'Orestie*. **1**: Roland Deville. **2**: André Steiger – Hubert Gignoux. **3**: André Roos. **5**: Théâtre National de Strasbourg. Strasbourg (France). 1969. *

4. – SOPHOCLES (496-406) – HEINER MÜLLER: *Philoctetes.*
1: Jürgen Rose. 2: Hans Lietzau. 5: Residenztheater.
München (Deutsches Schauspielhaus Hamburg) (BRD).
1968. 6: Rosemarie Clausen.

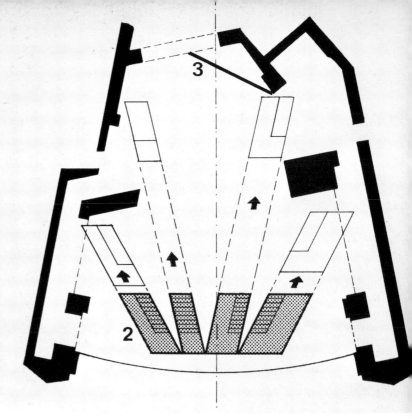

5   6

5/10. – SOPHOCLES (496-406) : *Oidipous Tyrannos – Antigonè.*
1 : Josef Svoboda. **2** : Otomar Krejca. **5** : Divadlo Za
Branou. Praha. 1971. **6** : Jaromir Svoboda.

7

8 9

10

11. — SOPHOCLES (496-406): *Antigonè*.
1: Helio Eichbauer. **2**: João Das Neves.
3: Geni Marcondes. **5**: Teatro Opinião.
Rio de Janeiro (Brasil). 1969. **6**: Carlos. *

12. — SOPHOCLES (496-406): *Antigonè*.
1: Sigurd Winge. **2**: Stein Winge.
5: Trondelag Teater. Trondheim (Norge).
1970. **6**: Roar Ohlander.

13. – SOPHOCLES (496-406) : *Antigonè*. **1** : Jozef Szajna.
2 : Olga Lipinska. **5** : Teatr Ludowy. Nowa Huta (Polska).
1963. **6** : Wojciech Plewinski.

14 | 16
15 |

14/17. – SOPHOCLES (496-406) – BERTOLT BRECHT - JUDITH MALINA : *Antigonè*. **1** : Julian Beck. **2** : Judith Malina – Julian Beck. **5** : The Living Theatre (New York). Krefeld (BRD). 1967. *

18. – SOPHOCLES (496-406) : *Oidipous Tyrannos*. **1** : Josef ▶ Svoboda. **2** : Miroslav Machacek. **5** : Narodni divadlo. Praha. 1963. **6** : Jaromir Svoboda.

17

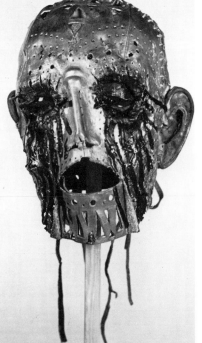

19/23. – SOPHOCLES (496-406) – FRIEDRICH HÖLDERLIN –
HEINER MÜLLER : *Oidipous Tyrannos*. **1** : Horst Sagert.
2 : Benno Besson. **3** : Reiner Bredemeyer. **4** : Brigitte
Soubeyran. **5** : Deutsches Theater. Berlin D.D.R. 1966.
6 : Gisela Brandt.

24/30. – SOPHOCLES (496-406) – FRIEDRICH HÖLDERLIN – HEINER MÜLLER : *Oidipous Tyrannos.* **1** : Horst Sagert. **2** : Benno Besson. **3** : Reiner Bredemeyer. **4** : Brigitte Soubeyran. **5** : Deutsches Theater. Berlin D.D.R. 1966. **6** : Cecilie Poetschukat.

24	25
	26
	27
	28
	29
	30

22

23

31. – SOPHOCLES (496-406): *Electra*. **1**: Ming Cho Lee. **2**: Gerald Freedman. **3**: John Morris. **5**: New York Shakespeare Festival. Delacorte Theater. New York (U.S.A.). 1964.

32. – EURIPIDES (480-406): *Troades*. **1**: Julio Prieto. **2**: Jose Sole. **3**: Leonardo Velazquez. **5**: Teatro Xola. Mexico. 1963.

33. – EURIPIDES (480-406) –
JEAN-PAUL SARTRE : *Troades*.
1 : Helio Eichbauer. **2** :
Paulo A. Grisolli. **5** : Teatro
Glaucio Gil. Rio de Janeiro
(Brasil). 1967. **6** : Carlos.

34. – EURIPIDES (480-406) :
Medeia. **1** : Ferry Barendse.
2 : Jo Dua. **5** : Koninklijke
Vlaamse Schouwburg.
Brussel. 1960.

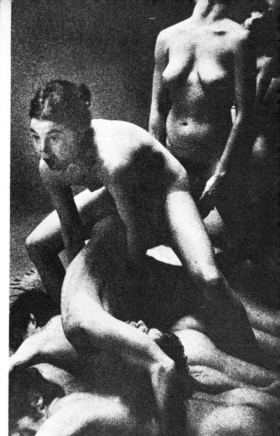

35 36

37

38

35/39. – EURIPIDES (480-406) – THE PERFORMANCE GROUP: *Bacchai* (*Dionysus in* 69). **1**: Michael Kirby – Jerry Rojo. **2**: Richard Schechner. **5**: The Performance Group. The Performing Garage. New York (U.S.A.). 1968. **6**: Frederick Eberstadt. *

40. – ARISTOPHANES (450-385): *Ornithes*. **1**: François Ganeau. **2**: Jacques Charron. **5**: Grand Théâtre de Genève. Genève (Helvetia). 1964. **6**: Vilém Sochurek.

41. – ARISTOPHANES (450-385) – PETER HACKS: *Eirènè*. **1**: Heinrich Kilger. **2**: Benno Besson. **3**: André Asriel. **4**: Brigitte Soubeyran. **5**: Deutsches Theater. Berlin D.D.R. 1962. **6**: Maria Steinfeldt.

42. – ARISTOPHANES (450-385): *Eirènè*. **1**: Fabian Puigsservet. **2**: Miguel Narros. **3**: Carmelo Bernaola. **5**: Teatro Español. Madrid. 1969. **6**: Gyenes.

43

43/45. — LUDOVICO ARIOSTO (1474-1533) — EDOARDO
SANGUINETI : *Orlando Furioso*. **1** : Uberto Bertacca – Elena
Nannini. **2** : Luca Ronconi. **5** : Teatro Libero di Roma.
Milano (Italia). 1970. **6** : Bernand. *

44   45

46/49. – *Arden of Faversham*. **1**: Drago Turina. **2**: Tomislav Radic. **5**: Zagrebacko dramsko pozoriste. Zagreb (Jugoslavija). 1969.

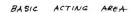

PROSCENIUM ARCH

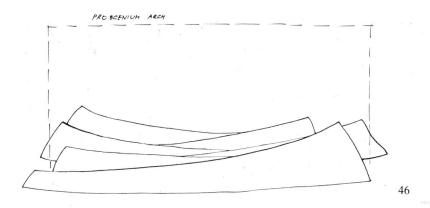

46

BASIC ACTING AREA

47

ARDEN'S HOUSE

48

49

FIELD , RIVER SIDE ETC.

SECTION PLAN

A

B
C

STAGE FLOOR

0   1   2   3   4   5   6   7   8   9   10   11 m

50. – WILLIAM SHAKESPEARE (1564-1616) – JOHN BARTON:
Wars of the Roses. **1**: John Bury. **2**: Peter Hall. **5**: Royal
Shakespeare Company. Stratford-on-Avon (U.K.). 1963.
6: Brook-Tella. *

51. – WILLIAM SHAKESPEARE (1564-1616): *Richard III*.
1: Jean-Denis Malclès. **2**: Jean Anouilh – Roland Pietri.
5: Théâtre Montparnasse–Gaston Baty. Paris. 1964.

52. – WILLIAM SHAKESPEARE (1564-1616) : Richard III.
1 : Eiji Tahara. 5 : Tokyo. 1965.

53. – WILLIAM SHAKESPEARE (1564-1616) : Romeo and Juliet.
1 : André Acquart. 2 : José Valverde. 5 : Théâtre Gérard
            Philipe. Saint-Denis (France). 1969.

54/57. – WILLIAM SHAKESPEARE (1564-1616): *Romeo and Juliet*. **1**: Kaoru Kanamori. **5**: Tokyo. 1970. **6**: Yoshiaki Hayashida. *

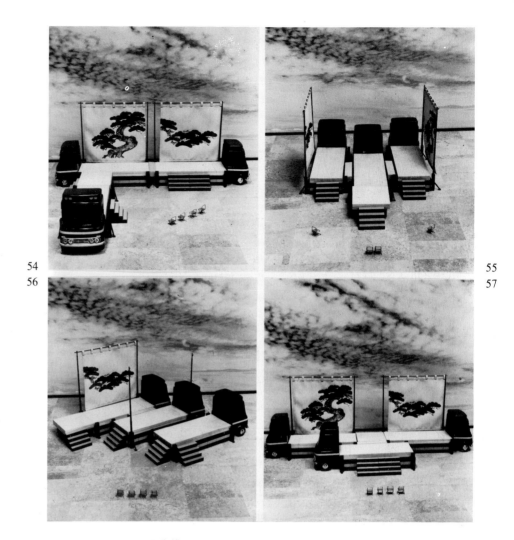

54
55
56
57

58. – WILLIAM SHAKESPEARE (1564-1616): *Romeo and Juliet*. **1**: Kesatoshi Shimizu. **5**: Tokyo. 1968.

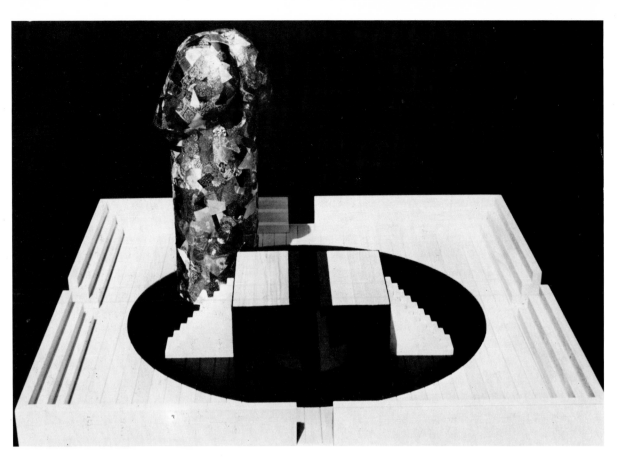

59. – WILLIAM SHAKESPEARE (1564-1616) : *Romeo and Juliet.*
1 : Ichirô Takada. 5 : Tokyo. 1971.

60. – WILLIAM SHAKESPEARE (1564-1616) : *Romeo and Juliet.*
1 : Josef Svoboda. 2 : Otomar Krejca. 5 : Narodni divadlo.
Praha. 1963. 6 : Jaromir Svoboda.

61/63. – WILLIAM SHAKESPEARE (1564-1616): *A Midsummer Night's Dream.* **1**: Sally Jacobs. **2**: Peter Brook. **3**: Richard Peaslee. **5**: Royal Shakespeare Company. Stratford-on-Avon (U.K.). 1970. **6**: David Farrell. *

61 62

63

64

64/67. – WILLIAM SHAKESPEARE (1564-1616) : *A Midsummer Night's Dream.* **1** : Sally Jacobs. **2** : Peter Brook. **3** : Richard Peaslee. **5** : Royal Shakespeare Company. Stratford-on-Avon (U.K.). 1970. **6** : David Farrell. *****

65

66

67

68. – WILLIAM SHAKESPEARE (1564-1616): *A Midsumm*
Night's Dream. **1**: Nicolaas Wijnberg. **2**: Han Ber
Van den Berg. **3**: Cor Lemaire. **4**: Albert M
5: Nederlandse Comedie. Stadsschouwburg. Amsterda
(Nederland). 1961. **6**: Lemaire.

69. – WILLIAM SHAKESPEARE (1564-1616): *A Midsumm*
Night's Dream. **1**: James D. Lyons, Jr. **2**: Phillip S. Johns
3: F. Richard Moore. **5**: Coleman Hall Theatre, Buckn
University. Lewisburg, Pennsylvania (U.S.A.). 19
6: James D. Lyons, Jr.

70. – WILLIAM SHAKESPEARE (1564-1616) – FRIEDRICH
DÜRRENMATT : *King John*. **1** : John Bogaerts. **2** : Walter
Tillemans. **5** : Koninklijke Nederlandse Schouwburg.
Antwerpen (België). 1969.

71. – WILLIAM SHAKESPEARE (1564-1616) : *The Merchant
of Venice*. **1** : Christian Egemar. **2** : Knut Thomassen.
5 : Den Nationale Scene. Bergen (Norge). 1969.
6 : Trygve Schönfelder.

72. – WILLIAM SHAKESPEARE (1564-1616): *Henry IV*.
1: Richard Prins – Kristian Fredrikson. **2**: John Sumner.
5. Melbourne Theatre Company. The Murdoch Court,
Victorian Arts Centre. Melbourne (Australia). 1969.
6: Graeme Harris.

74. – WILLIAM SHAKESPEARE (1564-1616): *As you like it.* ▶
1: Ralph Koltai. **2**: Clifford Williams. **5**: National
Theatre. London. 1967. **6**: Zoe Dominic. *

73. – WILLIAM SHAKESPEARE (1564-1616): *Julius Caesar*.
1: Nicholas Georgiadis. **2**: Minos Volanakis. **3**: Elisabeth
Lutyens. **5**: Old Vic. London. 1961. **6**: Philip Boukas.

75

76

78

77

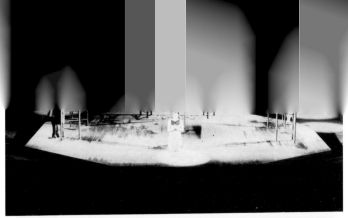

79
80

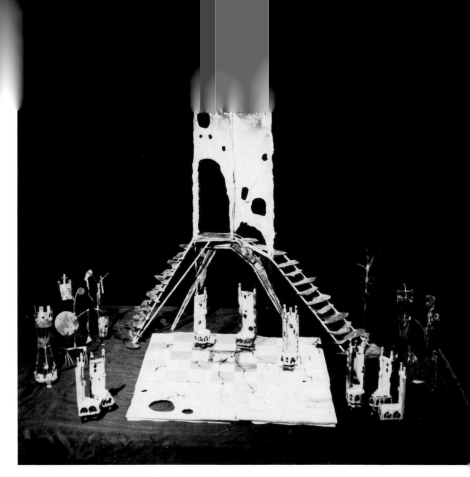

84. – WILLIAM SHAKESPEARE (1564-1616) : *Hamlet*. **1** : Jean Juillac. **2** : Maurice Sarrazin. **5** : Grenier de Toulouse. Toulouse (France). 1969.

81
82

79/83. – WILLIAM SHAKESPEARE (1564-1616) : *Hamlet*. **1** : Ichirô Takada. **2** : Toshikiyo Masumi. **5** : Haiyû-za. Tokyo – Osaka – Kyôto ... . 1971. **6** : Ichirô Takada.

85. – WILLIAM SHAKESPEARE (1564-1616) – HUMBERTO ORSINI : *La otra Historia de Hamlet*. **1** : Humberto Orsini. **2** : Humberto Orsini. **5** : Teatro Estudio 67. Caracas. 1967. **6** : Miguel Gracia.

83

86. – WILLIAM SHAKESPEARE (1564-1616) : *The merry Wives of Windsor*. **1** : Vladimir Marenic. **2** : Dejan Mijac. **5** : Srpsko narodno pozoriste. Novi Sad (Jugoslavija). 1966.
6 : Branko Cugelj.

87/88. – WILLIAM SHAKESPEARE (1564-1616): *Troilus and Cressida*. **1**: André Acquart. **2**: Roger Planchon. **3**: Claude Lochy. **5**: Théâtre de la Cité. Villeurbanne (France). 1964.

87

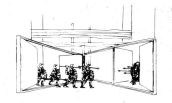

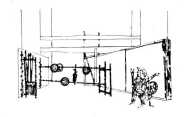

89. – WILLIAM SHAKESPEARE (1564-1616): *Measure for Measure.* **1**: William Underdown – Yannis Kokkos. **2**: Pierre Lefèvre. **3**: André Roos. **5**: Comédie de l'Est. Strasbourg (France). 1966. **6**: Michel Veilhan.

90. – WILLIAM SHAKESPEARE (1564-1616) – MARTIN SPERR: *Measure for Measure.* **1**: Wilfried Minks. **2**: Peter Zadek. **5**: Theater der Freien Hansestadt. Bremen (BRD). 1967. **6**: Günter Vierow.

91. – WILLIAM SHAKESPEARE (1564-1616) : *Othello*.
1 : Yasuhiro Mihara – Michiaki Ishida. **5** : Tokyo. 1969.

92. – WILLIAM SHAKESPEARE (1564-1616) : *Othello*. **1** : Jean-Michel Quesne. **2** : José Valverde. **3** : José Berghmans. **5** : Théâtre Gérard Philipe. Saint-Denis (France). 1971. **6** : Jacques Citles.

93. – WILLIAM SHAKESPEARE (1564-1616) : *Othello*. **1** : Alberto Sanchez. **2** : Alberto Sanchez. **5** : Teatro Universitario. Caracas. 1968. **6** : Donald Myerston.

95. – WILLIAM SHAKESPEARE (1564-1616): *King Lear*.
1: Yoshi Tosa. **2**: Robin Lovejoy. **5**: Old Tote Theatre
Company. Science Theatre, University of New South
Wales. Sydney (Australia). 1968. **6**: Robert Walker.

94. – WILLIAM SHAKESPEARE (1564-1616): *King Lear*.
1: Jacques Le Marquet. **2**: Georges Wilson. **5**: Théâtre
National Populaire. Paris. 1967. **6**: Birgit.

96. – WILLIAM SHAKESPEARE (1564-1616): *King Lear*.
1: Peter Brook. **2**: Peter Brook. **3**: Guy Woolfenden.
5: Royal Shakespeare Company. Stratford-on-Avon (U.K.).
1964. **6**: Gordon Goode.

97
98

99
100

97/100. – WILLIAM SHAKESPEARE (1564-1616): *Macbeth*. **1**: Otto Axer. **2**: Otto Axer. **5**: Teatr Polski. Warszawa. 1964. **6**: Otto Axer.

101. – WILLIAM SHAKESPEARE (1564-1616) – RICHARD SCHECHNER: *Makbeth (a collage derived from William Shakespeare's « Macbeth »)*. **1**: Jerry N. Rojo. **2**: Richard Schechner. **5**: The Performance Group. The Performing Garage. New York (U.S.A.). 1969.

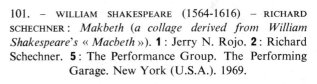

102/106. – WILLIAM SHAKESPEARE (1564-1616): *Macbeth.*
1: Rolf Stegars. **2**: Arvi Kivimaa. **3**: Heikki Aaltoila.
5: Suomen Kansallisteatteri. Helsinki. 1964.

102

103

104   105

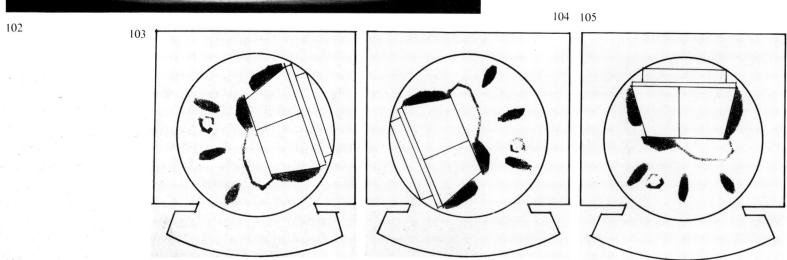

106

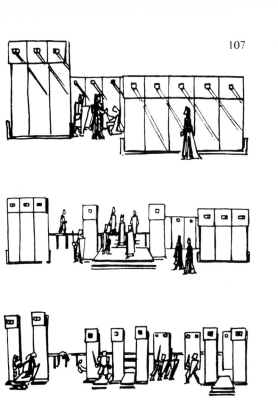

107/111. – WILLIAM SHAKESPEARE (1564-1616):
Macbeth. **1**: André Acquart. **2**: Guy Rétoré.
5: Théâtre de l'Est Parisien. Paris. 1965.

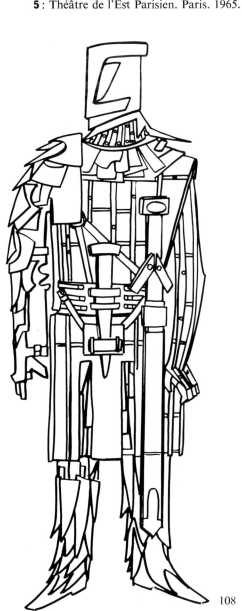

112

112/113. – WILLIAM SHAKESPEARE (1564-1616) – MAURICE MAETERLINCK – RAYMOND HERMANTIER : *Macbeth*. **1** : Ibou Diouf – Jean Philippe Abril – Line Senghor. **2** : Raymond Hermantier. **3** : Abdoulaye Diop. **5** : Compagnie d'Art Dramatique du Théâtre National Daniel Sorano. Dakar. 1969. **6** : Michel Renaudeau.

113

114

115

116
117

118
119

120

114/120. – WILLIAM SHAKESPEARE (1564-1616) – MAURICE MAETERLINCK – RAYMOND HERMANTIER : *Macbeth*. **1** : Ibou Diouf – Jean Philippe Abril – Line Senghor. **2** : Raymond Hermantier. **3** : Abdoulaye Diop. **5** : Compagnie d'Art Dramatique du Théâtre National Daniel Sorano. Dakar. 1969. **6** : Nicolas Treatt.

121/122. – WILLIAM SHAKESPEARE (1564-1616): *Macbeth*.
1: Eugene Lee. 2: Adrian Hall. 5: The Trinity Square
Repertory Company. Providence, Rhode Island (U.S.A.).
1969. 6: William L. Smith.

121

122

123

124

125

123/125. – WILLIAM SHAKESPEARE (1564-1616): *Macbeth.*
1: Liviu Ciulei. **2**: Liviu Ciulei. **5**: Teatrul Lucia Sturdza
Bulandra. Bucuresti. 1968. *

126

126/128. – WILLIAM SHAKESPEARE (1564-1616): *Antony and Cleopatra.* **1**: Jacques Marillier. **2**: François Maistre.**5**: Théâtre Sarah Bernhardt. Paris. 1964. **6**: Nicolas Treatt.

127

128

129

130
131

129/135. – WILLIAM SHAKESPEARE (1564-1616) – BERTOLT
BRECHT: *Coriolan*. **1**: Karl von Appen. **2**: Manfred
Wekwerth – Joachim Tenschert. **3**: Paul Dessau. **4**: Ruth
Berghaus. **5**: Berliner Ensemble. Berlin D.D.R. 1964.
6: Percy Paukschta.

132
133

135

134

136/138. – WILLIAM SHAKESPEARE (1564-1616): *Pericles, Prince of Tyre*. **1**: Timothy O'Brien. **2**: Terry Hands. **3**: Guy Woolfenden. **4**: John Broom. **5**: Royal Shakespeare Company. Stratford-on-Avon (U.K.). 1969. **6**: Reg Wilson.

139

140

141

142

143

141/143. – WILLIAM SHAKESPEARE (1564-1616) : *The Tempest*.
1 : Wilfried Minks. **2** : Klaus Michael Grüber. **5** : Theater
der Freien Hansestadt. Bremen (BRD). 1970.
6 : Günter Vierow.

144/145. – PEDRO CALDERON DE LA BARCA (1600-1681): *La Devocion de la Cruz.*
1: Bernard Floriet – Brigitte Tribouilloy – William Underdown. **2**: Alberto Rody. **5**: Comédie des Alpes. Maison de la Culture. Grenoble (France). 1969. **6**: Guy Delahaye.

144

145

146

147

146/148. – PEDRO CALDERON DE LA BARCA (1600-1681) –
JULIUSZ SLOWACKI – JERZY GROTOWSKI: *El Principe
constante*. **1**: Jerzy Gurawski – Wojciech Krygier. **2**: Jerzy
Grotowski. **5**: Teatr Laboratorium. Wroclaw (Polska).
1965.

148

149. – PIERRE CORNEILLE (1606-1684): *Le Menteur*. **1**: Bernard Floriet – Herat Sellner – Brigitte Tribouilloy. **2**: René Lesage. **5**: Comédie des Alpes. Maison de la Culture. Grenoble (France). 1970. **6**: Guy Delahaye.

150. – MOLIERE (1622-1673): *L'Ecole des Femmes*. **1**: Bernard Daydé. **2**: John Price. **5**: Det Kongelige Teater. Köbenhavn. 1970.

152 153

151/153. – MOLIERE (1622-1673): *Tartuffe*. **1**: Serghej
Barkhine. **2**: Iourij Lioubimov. **5**: Moskovskij Teatr
Dramy i Komedii na Taganke. Moskva. 1968.

154. – MOLIERE (1622-1673) : *Dom Juan*. **1** : Pierre Simonini.
2 : Pierre Dux. **5** : Théâtre de l'Œuvre. Paris. 1964.
6 : Pierre Simonini.

155. – MOLIERE (1622-1673) : *Dom Juan*. **1** : Vladimir
Marenic. **2** : Braslav Borozan. **5** : Narodno pozoriste.
Beograd. 1966. **6** : Branko Cugelj.

156. – MOLIERE (1622-1673) : *Dom Juan.*
1 : Gunter Kaiser. **2** : Benno Besson.
5 : Deutsches Theater. Berlin D.D.R. 1968.
6 : Gisela Brandt.

157. – MOLIERE (1622-1673) : *Dom Juan.* **1** : Jacques
Van Nerom. **2** : Jacques Joël. **5** : Théâtre Royal des Galeries.
Bruxelles. 1967.

158/159. – MOLIERE (1622-1673) : *Le Misanthrope*. **1** : Claude
Engelbach. **2** : Marcel Blüwal. **5** : Maison de la Culture.
Amiens (France). 1969.

158

159

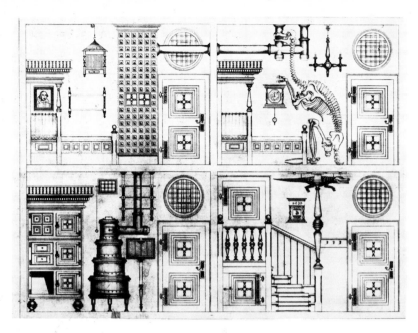

160. – MOLIERE (1622-1673): *L'Avare*. **1**: Wilfried Minks.
2: Peter Zadek. **5**: Theater der Freien Hansestadt.
Bremen (BRD). 1964. **6**: Günter Vierow.

161. – MOLIERE (1622-1673): *Le Bourgeois Gentilhomme*.
1: Nikolaj Dvigoubskij. **2**: Vladimir Shlesinger. **5**: Teatr
imeni Vakhtangova. Moskva. 1969.

162. – MOLIERE (1622-1673): *Le Malade imaginaire*.
1: Laszlo Szekely. **2**: Ferenc Daniel. **5**: Nemzeti Szinhaz.
Szeged (Magyarorszag). 1968. *

163/165. – JEAN RACINE (1639-1699): *Bérénice*. **1**: René
Allio. **2**: Roger Planchon. **5**: Théâtre de la Cité. Villeurbanne
(France). 1969. **6**: Etienne George – Nicolas Treatt. *

163

164

165

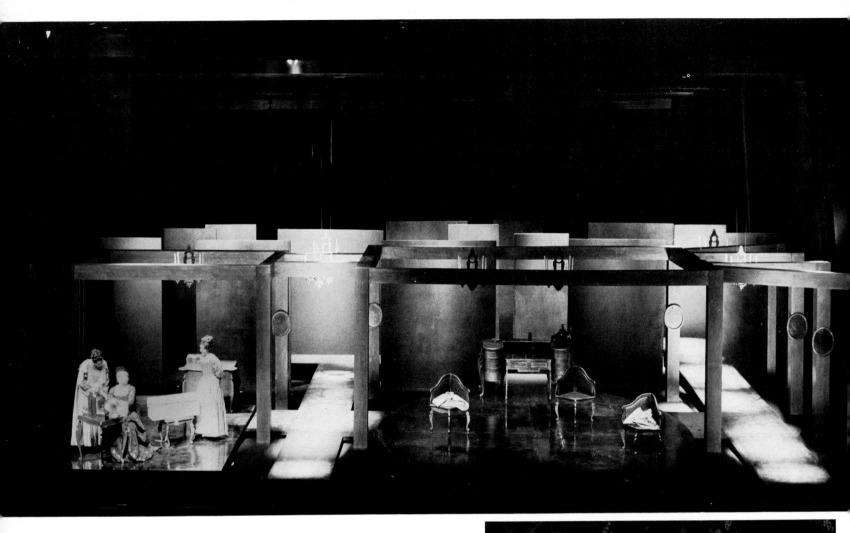

166. – ALAIN-RENÉ LESAGE (1668-1747): *Turcaret*. **1**: André
Acquart. **2**: Guy Rétoré. **5**: Théâtre de l'Est Parisien.
Paris. 1965.

167. – MARIVAUX (1688-1763): *La double Inconstance*.
1: Mimi Peetermans. **2**: Lode Verstraete. **5**: Koninklijke
Nederlandse Schouwburg. Antwerpen (België). 1969.

168. – MARIVAUX (1688-1763): *Le Prince travesti*.
1: Jo Tréhard – Girault. **2**: Jo Tréhard. **3**: Armand
Bex. **5**: Comédie de Caen. Caen (France). 1970.

169. – CARLO GOLDONI (1707-1793) – RAINER
WERNER FASSBINDER : *La Bottega del Caffè*.
1 : Wilfried Minks. **2** : Rainer Werner Fassbinder.
5 : Theater der Freien Hansestadt. Bremen
(BRD). 1969. **6** : Günter Vierow.

170. – CARLO GOLDONI (1707-1793) : *Baruffe chiozzotte*.
1 : Bernard Guillaumot. **2** : Jacques Lassalle. **3** : Blas
Sanchez. **4** : Michel Caserta. **5** : Studio Théâtre de Vitry.
Vitry (France). 1968.

171

172

173

171/173. – CARLO GOZZI (1720-1806) – MICHEL
ARNAUD : *Il Mostro turchino*. **1** : Jacques Noël.
2 : André Barsacq. **5** : Théâtre de l'Atelier.
Paris. 1966. **6** : Bernand.

174/178. – GOTTHOLD EPHRAIM LESSING (1729-1781):
Nathan der Weise. **1**: Heinrich Kilger. **2**: Friedo Solter.
5: Deutsches Theater. Berlin D.D.R. 1966
6: Cecilie Poetschukat.

174	176
	177
175	178

179. – JOHANN WOLFGANG GOETHE (1749-1832)
Torquato Tasso. **1**: Wilfried Minks. **2**: Peter Stein
5: Theater der Freien Hansestadt. Bremen (BRD)
1969. **6**: Günter Vierow.

180. – JOHANN WOLFGANG GOETHE (1749-1832) – FRIEDRICH
DÜRRENMATT : *Urfaust*. **1**: Michel Raffaëlli. **2**: Friedrich
Dürrenmatt. **5**: Schauspielhaus. Zürich (Helvetia). 1970.
6: Betty Raffaëlli.

181. – JOHANN WOLFGANG
GOETHE (1749-1832): *Faust I.*
1: Andreas Reinhardt –
Christine Stromberg. **2**: Adolf
Dresen – Wolfgang Heinz.
5: Deutsches Theater. Berlin
D.D.R. 1968. **6**: Maria Steinfeld.

182

183

182/183. – JOHANN WOLFGANG GOETHE (1749-1832):
Faust I. **1**: Andreas Reinhardt – Christine Stromberg.
2: Adolf Dresen – Wolfgang Heinz. **5**: Deutsches Theater.
Berlin D.D.R. 1968. **6**: Eva Stokowy.

184. – JOHANN WOLFGANG GOETHE (1749-1832): *Faust II.*
1 : Bernhard Heiliger. **2** : Ernst Schröder. **5** : Schiller Theater.
Berlin (West). 1966. **6** : Ilse Buhs.

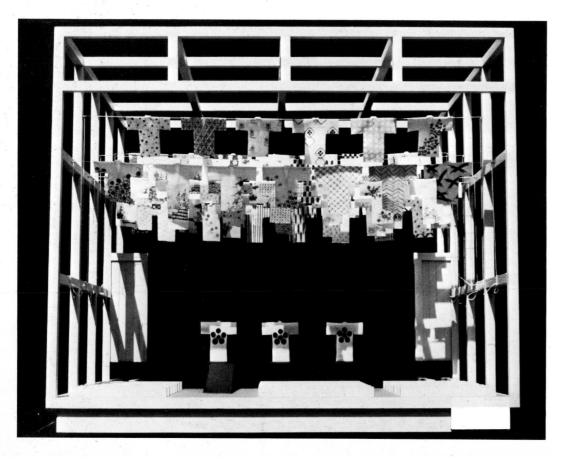

185. – NANBOKU TSURUYA (1755-1829) –
TADASHI SUZUKI: *Natsushibai, Howaito komedii.* **1** : Ichirô Takada. **2** : Tadashi Suzuki. **5** : Kizashi. Haiyûza-Gekijô. Tokyo. 1970.

186. – FRIEDRICH SCHILLER (1759-1805):
Die Räuber. **1**: Wilfried Minks. **2**: Peter
Zadek. **5**: Theater der Freien Hansestadt.
Bremen (BRD). 1966. **6**: Günter Vierow. *

187. – HEINRICH VON KLEIST (1777-1811): *Penthesilea*.
1: Ary Oechslin. **2**: Walter Oberer. **5**: Stadttheater.
Bern. 1968. **6**: Sandra Sibiglia.

188. – NIKOLAJ GOGOL (1809-1852) : *Revizor*. **1** : Lubos
Hruza. **2** : Jan Kacer. **5** : Cinoherni klub. Praha. 1967.
6 : Vilém Sochurek.

189. – JULIUSZ SLOWACKI (1809-1849) :
Kordian. **1** : Marian Kolodziej. **2** : Tadeusz
Minc. **5** : Teatr Nowy. Lodz (Polska). 1969.

190

191

190/191. – FEDOR DOSTOIEVSKIJ (1822-1881): *Peterbourgskie Snovedenia (Prestouplenie i Nakazanie)*. **1**: Alexandr Vassiliev. **2**: Yourij Zavadskij. **5**: Teatr Mossovieta. Moskva. 1969.

192. – HENRIK IBSEN (1828-1906): *Peer Gynt*. **1**: David
Sharir. **2**: Yossi Yzraely. **3**: Misha Segal. **4**: Yoram Boker.
5: Ha' Teatron Haleumi Habimah. Tel-Aviv. 1971
6: Jaacov Agor. *

193/194. – HENRIK IBSEN (1828-1906): *Brand.*
1 : Christian Egemar. **2** : Knut Thomassen. **5** : Den Nationale Scene. Bergen (Norge). 1968.
6 : Trygve Schönfelder.

193

194

195/197. – LAZA KOSTIC (1841-1910): *Maksim Crnojevic.*
1 : Miomir Denic. **2** : Arsa Jovanovic. **5** : Narodno pozoriste.
Beograd. 1967. **6** : Miroslav Krstic.

196 197

198. – AUGUST STRINDBERG (1849 – 1912) : *Dödsdansen*. **1** : Gunilla Palmstierna-Weiss. **2** :Ulf Palme. **5** : Dramatiska Teatern. Stockholm. 1967. **6** : Beata Bergström.

199. – AUGUST STRINDBERG (1849-1912): *Ett Drömspel*. **1** : Hubert Monloup. **2** : Raymond Rouleau. **5** : Comédie Française. Paris. 1970.

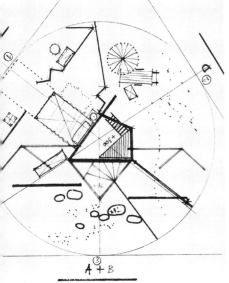

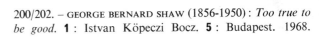

200/202. – GEORGE BERNARD SHAW (1856-1950): *Too true to be good.* **1** : Istvan Köpeczi Bocz. **5** : Budapest. 1968.

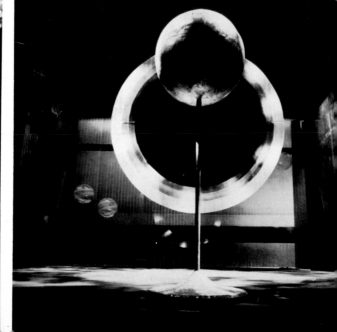

203/209. – GEORGE BERNARD SHAW (1856-1950): *Back to Methuselah*. **1**: Ralph Koltai. **2**: Clifford Williams. **3**: Marc Wilkinson. **5**: National Theatre. London. 1969. **6**: Anthony Crickmay/I.C.I. Plastics Division.

208

209

210/211. – ANTON TCHEKHOV (1860-1904): *Ivanov*. **1**: Josef Svoboda. **2**: Otomar Krejca. **5**: Divadlo Za Branou. Praha. 1970. **6**: Jaromir Svoboda.

211

212

212/213. – ANTON TCHEKHOV (1860-1904) : *Ivanov*. **1** : Arpad Csanyi. **2** : Endre Marton. **5** : Nemzeti Szinhaz. Budapest. 1971. *

213

214. – ANTON TCHEKHOV (1860-1904):
Vishnevyj Sad. **1**: Ferdinando Scarfiotti.
2: Luchino Visconti. **5**: Teatro Stabile di
Roma. Teatro Valle. Roma. 1966. **6**: Bosio.

215. – ANTON TCHEKHOV (1860-1904):
Vishnevyj Sad. **1**: Jürgen Rose. **2**: Hans
Lietzau. **5**: Deutsches Schauspielhaus.
Hamburg (BRD). 1970.
6: Rosemarie Clausen.

216. – RAMON MARIA DEL VALLE-INCLAN (1866-1936):
La Marquesa Rosalinda. **1**: Francisco Nieva. **2**: Miguel
Narros. 3: Manuel Angulo. **5**: Teatro Español. Madrid.
1970. **6**: Manuel Martinez Muñoz.

217

218

217/218. – PAUL CLAUDEL (1868-1955): *Protée*. **1**: Serge
Creuz. **2**: Georges Goubert. **5**: Maison de la Culture.
Rennes (France). 1970.

219/220. – MAXIM GORKIJ (1868-1936):
Na Dne. **1**: Libor Fara. **2**: Jan Kacer.
5: Cinoherni klub. Praha. 1971.
6: Vilém Sochurek.

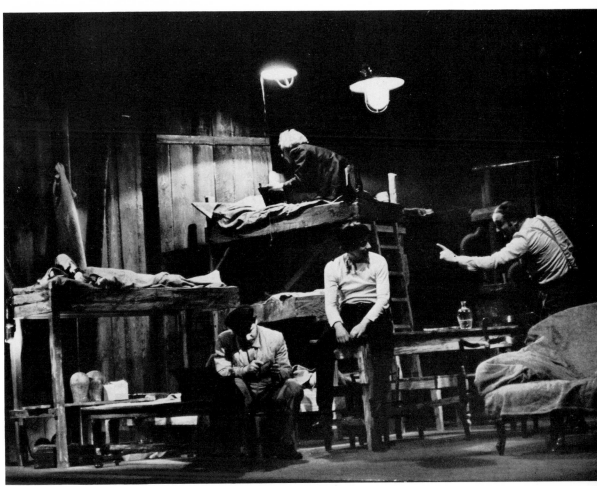

219

220

221. – MAXIM GORKIJ (1868-1936) : *Mat.* **1** : David Borovskij. **2** : Iourij Lioubimov. **5** : Moskovskij Teatr Dramy i Komedii na Taganke. Moskva. 1969.

222. – MAXIM GORKIJ (1868-1936) : *Poslednie.* **1** : André Acquart. **2** : André Steiger. **3** : André Roos. **5** : Théâtre National de Strasbourg (France). 1970. **6** : Michel Veilhan.

223/224. – STANISLAW WYSPIANSKI (1869-1907) – JERZY GROTOWSKI: *Akropolis*. **1**: Jozef Szajna – Jerzy Grotowski. **2**: Jozef Szajna – Jerzy Grotowski. **5**: Teatr Laboratorium 13 Rzedow. Opole (Polska). 1962. *

223

224

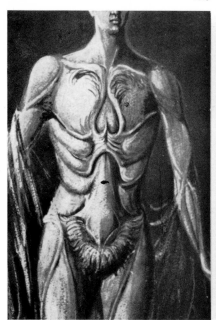

225/228. – ALFRED JARRY (1873-1907) – JEAN-LOUIS BARRAULT :
Jarry sur la Butte. **1** : Jacques Noël. **2** : Jean-Louis Barrault.
3 : Michel Legrand. **4** : Norbert Schmucki. **5** : Elysée –
Montmartre. Paris. 1970. **6** : Bernand.

228

229. – SEAN O'CASEY (1880-
1964) : *The Star turns red*.
1 : Yves-Bonnat. **2** : Pierre
Valde. **5** : Maison des
Jeunes et de la Culture.
Colombes (France). 1967.
6 : Nerval.

230. – ALEXEJ TOLSTOJ (1882-1945): *Smert Ivana Groznogo*. **1**: Iossif Soumbatashvili. **2**: Leonid Kheifits. **5**: Tsentralnyj Teatr Sovietskoj Armii. Moskva. 1966.

231. – JEAN GIRAUDOUX (1882-1944): *La Guerre de Troie n'aura pas lieu*. **1**: Kaoru Kanamori. **2**: Keita Asari. **5**: Gekidan – Shiki. Nissei Gekijô. Tokyo. 1969. **6**: Norihiko Matsumoto.

232

232/233. — STANISLAW
IGNACY WITKIEWICZ (1885-
1939): *Kurka Wodna*. **1**:
Tadeusz Kantor. **2**: Ta-
deusz Kantor. **5**: Teatr
Cricot 2. Krakow (Polska).
1967. **6**: Jan Poplonski –
Henryk Makarewicz –
Jacek Stoklosa.

233

234

235

236

234/236. – STANISLAW IGNACY WITKIEWICZ (1885-1939):
Wariat i Zakonnica. **1**: Tadeusz Kantor. **2**: Tadeusz
Kantor. **5**: Teatr Cricot 2. Krakow (Polska). 1963. **6**:
Waclaw Nowak – Jerzy Borowiec.

237. – STANISLAW
IGNACY WITKIE-
WICZ (1885-1939):
Bezimienne Dzieła
1 : Marian Ko-
lodziej. **2**: Zbig-
niew Bogdanski.
5 : Teatr Wybrze-
ze. Gdansk
(Polska). 1968.
6 : Tadeusz Link

238. – STANISLAW
IGNACY
WITKIEWICZ
(1885-1939):
Matka. **1** : Marian
Kolodziej. **2** :
Tadeusz Minc.
5 : Teatr
Wybrzeze.
Gdansk (Polska).
1969.
6 : Tadeusz Link

239

240

239/241. – JOHN REED (1887-1920): *Ten Days that shook the World*. **1**: Alexandr Tarassov. **2**: Iourij Lioubimov. **5**: Moskovskij Teatr Dramy i Komedii na Taganke. Moskva. 1965.

241

242

242/244. – OSWALDO DE ANDRADE (1890-1954): *O Rei da Vela*.
1 : Helio Eichbauer. **2** : Jose Celso C. Martinez. **5** : Teatro
Oficina. São Paulo (Brasil). 1967. *

243   244

245. – OSWALDO DE ANDRADE (1890-1954) :
O Rei da Vela. **1** : Jorge Carrozzino –
Carmen Prieto. **2** : Bernardo Galli. **5** : El
Galpon. Montevideo. 1969.
6 : Christian Griffoul.

246. – LUCIAN BLAGA (1895-1961):
Mesterul Manole. **1** : Sanda Musatescu.
2 : Dinu Cernescu. **5** : Teatrul Giulesti.
Bucuresti. 1968. *

247. – EVGHENI SCHWARZ (1896-1958):
Drakon. **1** : Michel Raffaëlli. **2** : Antoine
Vitez. **3** : André Chamoux. **5** : Comédie
de Saint-Etienne. Maison de la Culture
de Grenoble. Grenoble (France). 1968.
6 : Betty Raffaëlli.

248

249

250

248/254. – EVGHENI SCHWARZ (1896-1958): *Drakon*.
1 : Horst Sagert. **2** : Benno Besson. **3** : Reiner Bredemeyer.
4 : Brigitte Soubeyran. **5** : Deutsches Theater. Berlin D.D.R.
1965. **6** : Gisela Brandt.

251	252
253	254

255. – TAWFIK EL-HAKIM (1898): *Maglis al A'dl*. **1**: Ramzi Mostafa. **2**: Ramzi Mostafa. **5**: Al Masrah al Hadis. Al Gaama al Amrikia. Al Kahira (Cairo). 1971.

256. – WILHELM MOBERG (1898): *Domaren*. **1**: Rolf Stegars. **2**: Edvine Laine. **5**: Suomen Kansallisteatteri. Helsinki. 1963. **6**: Kari Hakli. *

257. – BERTOLT BRECHT (1898-1956): *Die Drei-groschenoper*. **1**: Franciszka Themerson. **2**: Michael Meschke. **3**: Kurt Weill. **4**: Holger Rosenquist. **5**: Marionetteatern. Stockholm. 1967. **6**: Sven-Göran Drejhammar.

258. – BERTOLT BRECHT (1898-1956): *Die Drei-groschenoper*. **1**: Eduardo Arrocha. **2**: Nestor Raimondi. **3**: Kurt Weill. **5**: La Habana. 1967. **6**: Christian Griffoul.

259. – BERTOLT BRECHT (1898-1956): *Die Drei-groschenoper*. **1**: Serge Creuz. **2**: Anton Peters. **3**: Kurt Weill. **5**: Koninklijke Vlaamse Schouwburg. Brussel. 1969.

260. – BERTOLT BRECHT (1898-1956): *Die Drei-groschenoper*. **1**: Jorge Carrozzino – Carmen Prieto. **2**: Atahualpa del Cioppo. **3**: Kurt Weill. **5**: El Galpon. Montevideo. 1970. **6**: Christian Griffoul.

258   259   260

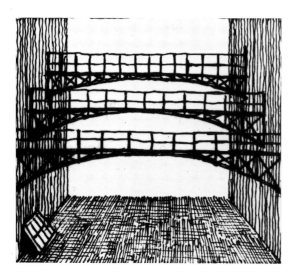

261/266. – BERTOLT BRECHT (1898-1956): *Die heilige Johanna der Schlachthöfe*. **1**: Karl von Appen. **2**: Manfred Wekwerth – Joachim Tenschert. **3**: Hans-Dieter Hosalla. **5**: Berliner Ensemble. Berlin D.D.R. 1968. **6**: Maria Steinfeldt – Percy Paukschta.

261	265
262	
263	266
264	

267/268. – BERTOLT BRECHT (1898-1956): *Die Ausnahme und die Regel*. **1**: Richard Montgomery. **2**: Sam Walters. **5**: Little Theatre. Kingston (Jamaica – West Indies). 1970. **6**: Richard Montgomery.

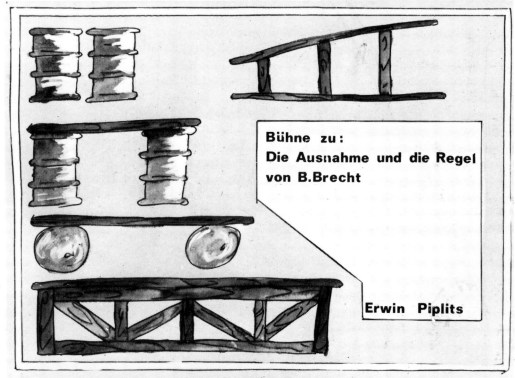

Bühne zu:
Die Ausnahme und die Regel
von B.Brecht

Erwin Piplits

269/270. – BERTOLT BRECHT (1898-1956): *Die Ausnahme und die Regel*. **1**: Erwin Piplits. **2**: Sinn Paulsen. **5**: Gladsaxe Teater. Köbenhavn. 1970.

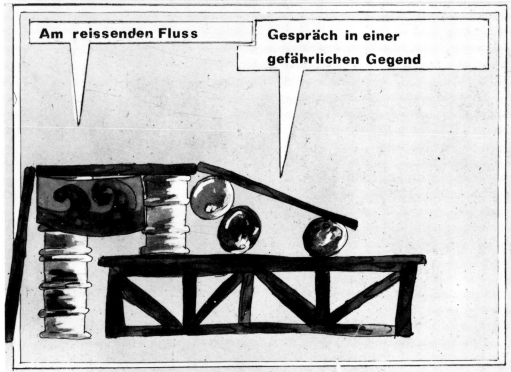

Am reissenden Fluss

Gespräch in einer gefährlichen Gegend

271

271/273. – BERTOLT BRECHT (1898-1956): *Leben des Galilei.*
1: Jost Assman. 2: Torsten Sjöholm. 3: Arne Rasset.
5: Stadsteatern. Norrköping – Linköping (Sverige). 1970.
6: Anders Mattsson.

272

273

274/277. – BERTOLT BRECHT (1898-1956) : *Leben des Galilei.*
1 : Enar Stenberg. **2** : Iourij Lioubimov. **5** : Moskovskij
Teatr Dramy i Komedii na Taganke. Moskva. 1966.

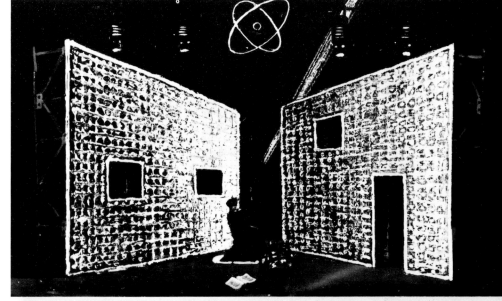

275

276

74

277

278. – BERTOLT BRECHT (1898-1956): *Der gute Mensch von Sezuan*. **1**: Achim Freyer. **2**: Benno Besson. **3**: Paul Dessau. **5**: Volksbühne. Berlin D.D.R. 1970. **6**: Harry Hirschfeld. *

279. – BERTOLT BRECHT (1898-1956): *Der gute Mensch von Sezuan*. **1**: Niels Hamel. **2**: Erik Vos. **3**: Cor Lemaire. **5**: Theater. Stadsschouwburg. Nijmegen (Nederland). 1968. **6**: Wouter van Heusden.

280. – BERTOLT BRECHT (1898-1956):
Der gute Mensch von Sezuan. **1**: Douglas
W. Schmidt – Carrie F. Robbins.
2: Robert Symonds. **5**: Repertory
Theater of Lincoln Center. The Vivian
Beaumont Theater. New York (U.S.A.).
1970. **6**: Martha Swope.

281. – BERTOLT BRECHT (1898-1956):
Der gute Mensch von Sezuan. **1**: Sakina
Mohamed Ali. **2**: Saad Ardash. **5**: Masrah
al Hakim. Al Kahira (Cairo). 1967.
6: Nagi Yassa.

282/284. – BERTOLT BRECHT (1898-1956):
Herr Puntila und sein Knecht Matti. **1** : Iossif
Soumbatashvili. **2** : Horst Havemann. **5** :
Tsentralnyj Teatr Sovietskoj Armii. Moskva.
1966. **6** : Vilém Sochurek.

282

283

284

285. – BERTOLT BRECHT
(1898-1956) : *Herr Puntila
und sein Knecht Matti.*
1 : Murray Laufer. **2** :
Kurt Reis. **5** : St Lawrence
Centre. Toronto (Canada).
1971. **6** : David Leigh.

286. – BERTOLT BRECHT (1898-1956): *Schweyk im zweiten Weltkrieg*. **1**: Wilfried Minks. **2**: Peter Palitzsch. **5**: Theater der Freien Hansestadt. Bremen (BRD). 1968. **6**: Günter Vierow.

287. – BERTOLT BRECHT (1898-1956): *Der kaukasische Kreidekreis*. **1**: Ary Œchslin. **2**: Günther Buch. **5**: Stadttheater. Bern. 1971. **6**: Willi Gasché.

288. – IGNAZIO SILONE (1900): *L'Avventura d'un povero Cristiano*. **1**: Alberto Burri. **2**: Valerio Zurlini. **3**: Mario Zafred. **5**: Teatro Stabile dell'Aquila. Aquila (Italia). 1969.

289/290. – NELSON RODRIGUES (1900): *Album de Familia*. **1**: Helio Eichbauer. **2**: Martim Gonçalves. **5**: Teatro Ateneo. Caracas. 1968. **6**: Miro Anton.

289

290

291. – HALLDOR LAXNESS (1902) : *Prjonastofan Solin.*
1 : Gunnar Bjarnason. **2** : Baldvin Halldorsson.
5 : Pjodleikhusid. Reykjavik. 1966.
6 : Ljosmyndastafa Oli Pall.

292. – NIKOLAJ OSTROVSKI (1904-1936) :
Kak zakalialas Stal. **1** : Aïmi Ounz. **2** : Mikk
Mikiver. **5** : Molodejnyj Teatr. Tallinn
(S.S.S.R.). 1968.

293. – JEAN-PAUL SARTRE
(1905) : *Le Diable et le
Bon Dieu.* **1** : André
Acquart. **2** : Georges
Wilson. **5** : Théâtre
National Populaire.
Paris. 1968.

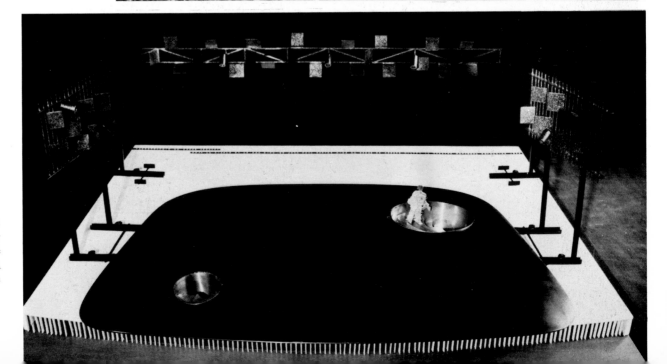

294. – GHEORGHIJ MDIVANI (1905): *Den Rojdeniia Terezy.*
1: Iossif Soumbatashvili. **2**: Boris Ravenskikh. **5**: Teatr
Poushkina. Moskva. 1961.

295. – SAMUEL BECKETT (1906): *En attendant Godot.*
1: Stephen Hendrickson. **2**: Meredith Dallas. **5**: Antioch
Area Theatre. Yellow Springs, Ohio (U.S.A.). 1966. *

296/298. – SAMUEL BECKETT (1906): *En attendant Godot.*
1: Igael Tumarkin. **2**: Yossi Yzraely. **3**: Misha Segal.
5: Ha'Teatron Haleumi Habimah. Tel-Aviv. 1968.
6: Jaacov Agor.

296

297

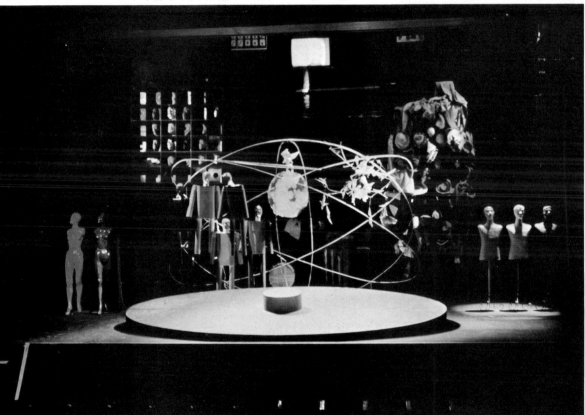

298

300

299/300. – ALEXEJ ARBOUZOV (1908): *Moj biednyj Marat.*
1: Margarita Moukosseeva. **2**: Leonid Kheifits. **5**:
Tsentralnyj Teatr Sovietskoj Armii. Moskva. 1965.

301. – LEONID MALIOUGHINE (1909-1968): *Moe nasmechlivoe
Stchastie.* **1**: Edouard Kotcherghine. **2**: Rouben
Agamirzian – Kame Ghinkas. **5**: Teatr imeni
Komissarjevskoy. Leningrad (S.S.S.R.). 1968.

302. – JEAN ANOUILH (1910): *Antigone*. **1**: Donald
Oenslager – Gordon Micunis. **2**: Jerome Kilty. **3**: John
Duffy. **5**: American Shakespeare Festival.
Stratford, Connecticut (U.S.A.). 1967. *

303. – JEAN ANOUILH
(1910): *Le Boulanger, la
Boulangère et le petit
Mitron*. **1**: Jean-Denis
Malclès. **2**: Jean Anouilh –
Roland Pietri. **5**: Comédie
des Champs-Elysées.
Paris. 1968.

304. – JEAN GENET (1910): *Les Bonnes*. **1**: Claude Engelbach. **2**: Roland Monod. **5**: Comédie de Saint-Etienne. Saint-Etienne (France). 1971. **6**: Marisa Duhalde.

307. – JEAN GENET (1910): *Le Balcon*. ▶ **1**: Helio Eichbauer. **2**: Martim Gonçalves. **5**: Teatro João Caetano. Rio de Janeiro (Brasil). 1970. **6**: Carlos.

308. – JEAN GENET (1910): *Le Balcon*. **1**: J.S. Ostoja-Kotkowski. **2**: Wal Cherry. **5**: Adelaide University Theatre Guild. University Union Hall. Adelaide (Australia). 1965. * ▶

305/306. – JEAN GENET (1910): *Les Bonnes*. **1**: Victor Garcia – Enrique Alarcon. **2**: Victor Garcia. **5**: Nuria Espert. Teatro Poliorama. Barcelona (España). 1968. **6**: Bernand.

305 306

309/313. — JEAN GENET (1910): *Les Paravents*. **1** : Jürgen Rose. **2** : Hans Lietzau. **5** : Residenztheater. München (BRD). 1968.

309

310	311
312	313

314

314/315. – JEAN GENET (1910): *Les Paravents*. **1**: André
Acquart. **2**: Roger Blin. **5**: Compagnie Renaud – Barrault.
Odéon – Théâtre de France. Paris. 1966.

315

316. – MAX FRISCH (1911): *Don Juan oder Die Liebe zur Geometrie.*
1: Valerij Levental. **2**: Valentin Ploutchek. **5**: Teatr Satiry. Moskva. 1966. Vilém Sochurek.

317. – MAX FRISCH (1911): *Andorra.* **1**: Rudolf Schneider – Manns – Au. **2**: Leon Epp. **5**: Volkstheater. Wien. 1962.

318/321. – EUGENE IONESCO (1912): *Le Piéton de l'Air.*
1: Jacques Noël. **2**: Jean-Louis Barrault. **5**: Compagnie
Renaud – Barrault. Odéon – Théâtre de France. Paris. 1963.

319

320

318

321

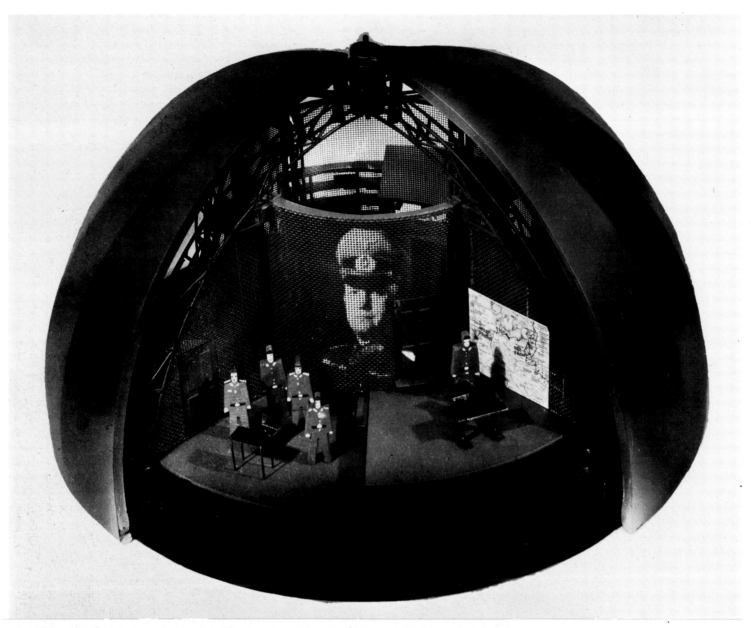

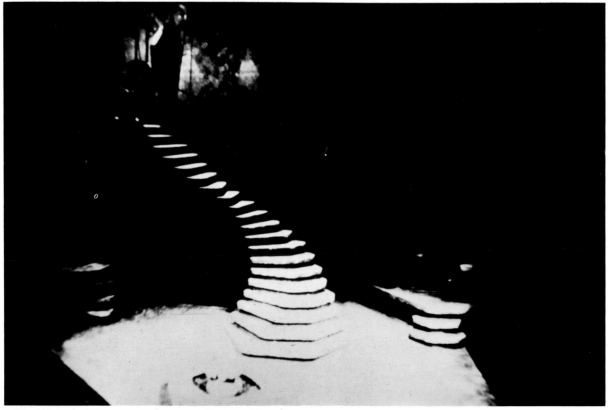

322. – HANS HELLMUT KIRST (1914)–ERWIN PISCATOR: *Aufstand der Offiziere*. **1**: Hans-Ulrich Schmückle. **2**: Erwin Piscator. **3**: Aleida Montijn. **5**: Freie Volksbühne. Berlin (West). 1966. **6**: Heinrich Fürtinger. *

323. – TENNESSEE WILLIAMS (1914): *Camino Real*. **1**: Peter Wexler. **2**: Milton Katselas. **5**: Center Theater Group of the Mark Taper Forum. Los Angeles, California (U.S.A.). 1968.

324. – TORE ZETTERHOLM (1915): *Kvinnorna fran Shanghai.*
1: Christian Egemar. **2**: Sigmund Saeverud. **5**: Den
Nationale Scene. Bergen (Norge). 1968.
6: Trygve Schönfelder.

325. – ARTHUR MILLER (1915): *The Crucible.* **1**: Manuel
Barreiro. **2**: Gilda Hernandez. **5**: Grupo Taller Dramatico.
Teatro Mella. La Habana. 1968. **6**: Christian Griffoul.

326. – ARTHUR MILLER (1915): *After the Fall.* **1**: Jo
Mielziner. **2**: Edward Parone. **5**: Martin Tahse Production
presented by the American National Theatre and Academy
(Touring Company). The Playhouse. Wilmington, Delaware
(U.S.A.). 1964. **6**: Peter Juley. *

327

327/331. – TADEUSZ HOLUJ (1916): *Puste Pole*. **1**: Jozef Szajna. **2**: Jozef Szajna. **5**: Teatr Ludowy. Nowa Huta (Polska). 1965. **6**: Wojciech Plewinski. *

328

329

30

31

AKCJA W DOLE I NA GÓRZE SCENY

⑦ scena pogrzebu Adasia – stukot chodaków. więźniów!. marsz

133

332. – PETER WEISS (1916): *Die Ermittlung*. **1**: Gunilla Palmstierna – Weiss. **2**: Ingmar Bergman. **5**: Dramatiska Teatern. Stockholm. 1966. **6**: Beata Bergström.

333. – PETER WEISS (1916): *Die Ermittlung*. **1**: Hans-Ulrich Schmückle. **2**: Erwin Piscator. **3**: Luigi Nono. **5**: Freie Volksbühne. Berlin (West). 1965. **6**: Heinz Köster.

DIE ERMITTLUNG

SZENISCHES ORATORIUM

IN 11 GESÄNGEN

334. – PETER WEISS (1916): *Die Verfolgung und Ermordung Jean Paul Marats, dargestellt durch die Schauspielgruppe des Hospizes zu Charenton, unter Anleitung des Herrn de Sade.* **1**: Peter Weiss. **2**: Conrad Swinarski. **4**: Deryk Mendel. **5**: Schiller Theater. Berlin (West). 1964. **6**: Harry Croner.

335/336. – PETER WEISS (1916): *Die Verfolgung und Ermordung Jean Paul Marats, dargestellt durch die Schauspielgruppe des Hospizes zu Charenton, unter Anleitung des Herrn de Sade.* **1**: Gunilla Palmstierna – Weiss. **2**: Frank Sundström. **5**: Dramatiska Teatern. Stockholm. 1965. **6**: Beata Bergström. *

337. – PETER WEISS (1916): *Die Verfolgung und Ermordung Jean Paul Marats, dargestellt durch die Schauspielgruppe des Hospizes zu Charenton, unter Anleitung des Herrn de Sade.* **1**: Christian Egemar. **2**: Otto Homlung. **5**: Den Nationale Scene. Bergen (Norge). 1970. **6**: Trygve Schönfelder.

335

337   336

338. – PETER WEISS (1916): *Gesang vom lusitanischen Popanz.*
1: Waltraut Mau – Ilse Träbing – Klaus Weiffenbach.
2: Karl Paryla. **5**: Schaubühne am Halleschen Ufer.
Berlin (West). 1967. **6**: Harry Croner.

339. – PETER WEISS (1916): *Gesang vom lusitanischen Popanz.*
1: Gunilla Palmstierna – Weiss.
5: Scala Teatern. Stockholm. 1968.

340. – PETER WEISS (1916):
*Gesang vom lusitanischen
Popanz.* **1**: Samir Ahmed.
2: Ahmed Zaki. **5**: Masrah
al Geib. Al Kahira (Cairo).
1971. **6**: Samir Azmi.

341/342. – PETER WEISS (1916): *Vietnam Diskurs.*
1: Gunilla Palmstierna – Weiss. 2: Harry
Buckwitz. 5: Städtische Bühnen. Frankfurt
(BRD). 1968. 6: Günter Englert.

341

342

343. – PETER WEISS (1916): *Vietnam Diskurs.* 1: Setsu
Asakura. 2: Tatsuji Iwabuchi. 5: Haiyû - za. Haiyûza-
Gekijô. Tokyo. 1968. 6: Shigeko Higuchi.

344. – BERT SCHIERBEEK (1918): *Een groot doo...*
Dier. **1**: Karel Appel. **2**: Kees Van Ierse...
3: Jan Boerman – Dick Raaijmakers. **5**: Stud...
en het Holland Festival. Grand Théâtre Gooiland...
Hilversum (Nederland). 1963. **6**: Maria Austri...

345. – JEAN SIGRID (1920): *Quoi de neuf, Arus...*
1: Raymond Renard. **2**: Pierre Larc...
5: Théâtre du Rideau de Bruxelles. Bruxe...
1970. **6**: Oscar.

346. – NORMAN FREDERICK SIMPSON (1920): *One-Way Pendulum*. **1**: Hugoke. **2**: Lode Hendrickx. **5**: Koninklijke Nederlandse Schouwburg. Antwerpen (België). 1963.

347. – AGUSTIN CUZZANI (1920): *Una Libra de Carne*. **1**: Vladimir Serebrovskij. **2**: Vladimir Andreev. **5**: Teatr imeni Ermolovoj. Moskva. 1965.

348. – ARIANO SUASSUNA (1920): *O Auto da Compadecida*. **1**: Walter Wallbaum. **2**: Friedo Solter. **5**: Kammerspiele des Deutschen Theaters. Berlin D.D.R. 1968. **6**: Erich Seidenstricker.

349. – EJI STAVINSKI (1921): *Tchas Pik*. **1**: David Borovskij. **2**: Iourij Lioubimov. **5**: Moskovskij Teatr Dramy i Komedii na Taganke. Moskva. 1969. **6**: Christian Griffoul.

350. – BENJAMIN GALAI (1921): *Sippur Uriah*. **1**: Gila Schakhine. **2**: Oded Kotler. **3**: Yehezkiel Braun. **5**: Bamat Hasachkanim. Tel-Aviv. 1967. **6**: Jaacov Agor. *

351. – MUSTAFA MAHMOUD (1921): *Al Insan Wal Zil*. **1**: Samir Zaki. **2**: Hassan Abd El Salam. **5**: Masrah al Geib. Al Kahira (Cairo). 1970. **6**: Mostafa Dessouki.

352. – TADEUSZ ROZEWICZ (1921):
Stara Kobieta wysiaduje. **1**: Wojciech
Krakowski. **2**: Jerzy Jarocki. **5**: Teatr
Wspolczesny. Wroclaw (Polska). 1969.
6: Grazyna Wyszomirska.

353. – WOLFGANG BORCHERT (1921-
1947): *Draussen vor der Tür*. **1**: Algis
Mikenas. **2**: Juozas Miltinis. **3**:
Edouardas Balsys. **5**: Dramoteatras.
Panevezys (S.S.S.R.). 1967.
6: Kazys Vitkus.

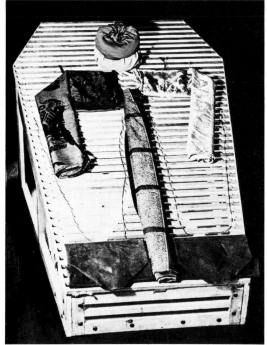

354

355

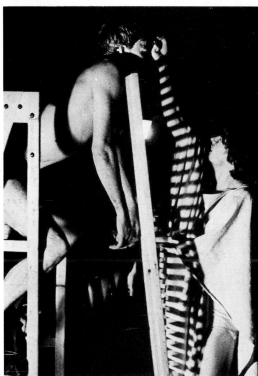

357

356

354/358. – OLE SARVIG (1921): *Kaspariana*. **1**: Eugenio Barba – Bernt Nyberg. **2**: Eugenio Barba. **5**: Odin Teatret. Holstebro (Danmark). 1967. **6**: Roald Pay – Delta. *

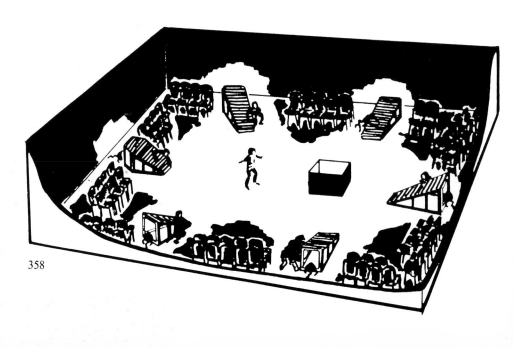

358

359. – FRIEDRICH DÜRRENMATT (1921): *Die Wiedertaüfer*.
1: Josef Svoboda. **2**: Miroslav Machacek. **5**: Narodni
Divadlo. Praha. 1968. **6**: Jaromir Svoboda.

360. – FRIEDRICH DÜRRENMATT (1921): *Die Wiedertaüfer*.
1: René Allio. **2**: André Steiger. **3**: André Roos. **5**: Théâtre
National de Strasbourg. Strasbourg (France). 1969.
6: Michel Veilhan.

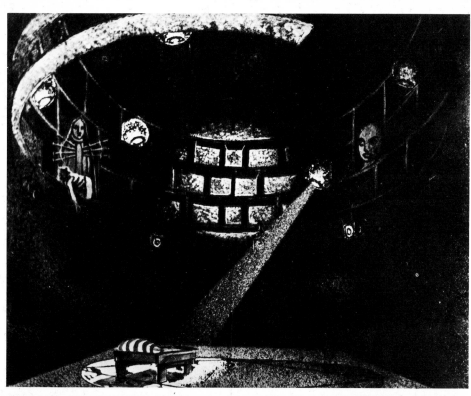

361. – IONAS AVIJUS (1922): *V Vikhre*. **1**: Felix Navitskas.
2: Ghenrikos Vantsiavitchus. **5**: Gosoudarstvennyj
Akademitcheskij Teatr Dramy. Vilnius (S.S.S.R.). 1970.

362. – LUIGI SQUARZINA (1922): *Emmeti*. **1**: Gianni Polidori.
2: Luigi Squarzina. **5**: Teatro Stabile. Genova (Italia). 1966.
6: Francesco Leoni.

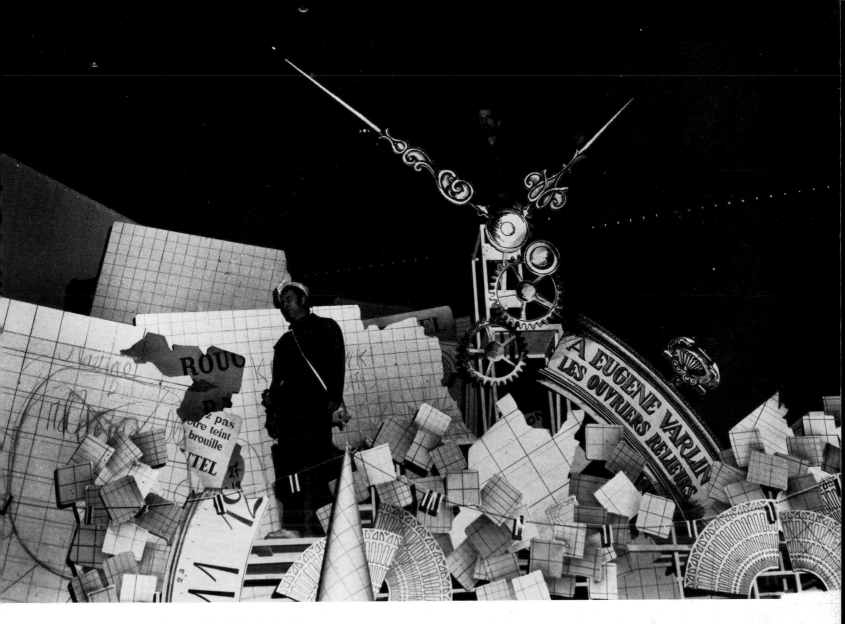

363. – ARMAND GATTI (1924): *Les 13 Soleils de la Rue Saint Blaise*. **1** : Hubert Monloup. **2** : Guy Rétoré. **3** : Diego Masson. **5** : Théâtre de l'Est Parisien. Paris. 1968. **6** : Samy Poliatchek.

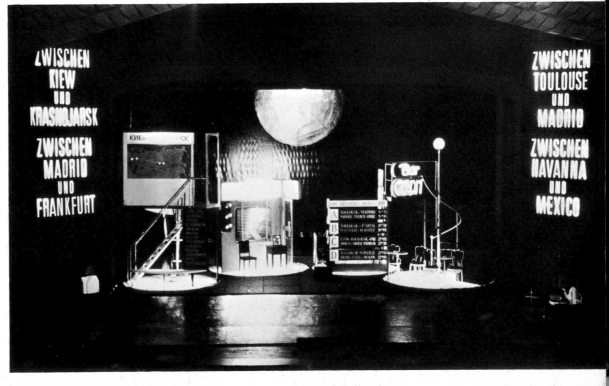

364. – ARMAND GATTI (1924). *La Passion selon Franco*. **1** : Michel Raffaëlli. **2** : Kaï Braak. **3** : Michel Raffaëlli. **5** : Staatstheater. Kassel (BRD). 1967.

365. – JIRI SOTOLA (1924): *Antiorfeus*. **1**: Vladimir Nyvlt. **2**: Frantisek Stepanek. **5**: Divadlo na Vinohradech. Praha. 1965. **6**: Vilém Sochurek.

366

366/367. – PETER SEEBERG (1925): *Ferai*. **1**: Eugenio Barba – Iben Nagel Rasmussen – Jacob Jensen. **2**: Eugenio Barba. **5**: Odin Teatret. Holstebro (Danmark). 1969. **6**: Odin Teatret. *

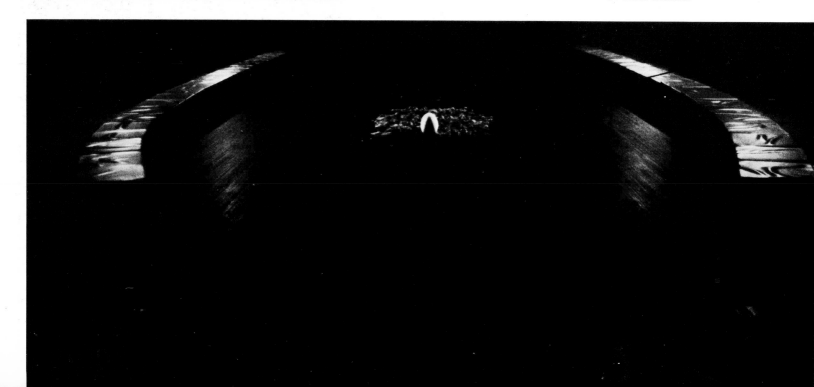

368/369. – JAMES SAUNDERS (1925): *Dog Accident.* **2**: Ed Berman. **5**: Ambiance Lunch–Hour Theatre Club. In the open-air at Marble Arch. London. 1969. **6**: Brian Pollard. *

368	369
	370

370. – JAIME SALOM (1925): *Los Delfines.* **1**: Sigfrido Burman. **2**: José Maria Loperena. **5**: Compañia Titular del Teatro Nacional de la Ciudad de Barcelona " Calderon de la Barca ". Teatro Calderon de la Barca. Barcelona (España). 1969. **6**: Gyenes.

371. – HERMANN KANT (1926): *Die Aula*. **1**: Frank Borisch. **2**: Lothar Schneider. **5**: Bühnen der Stadt. Magdeburg. D.D.R. 1969. **6**: Dewag.

372. – CARLOS MUÑIZ (1927): *El Tintero*. **1**: Jacobo Borges. **2**: Eduardo Moreno. **5**: Teatro ACAT. Valencia (Venezuela). 1965. **6**: Hector Lopez Orihuela.

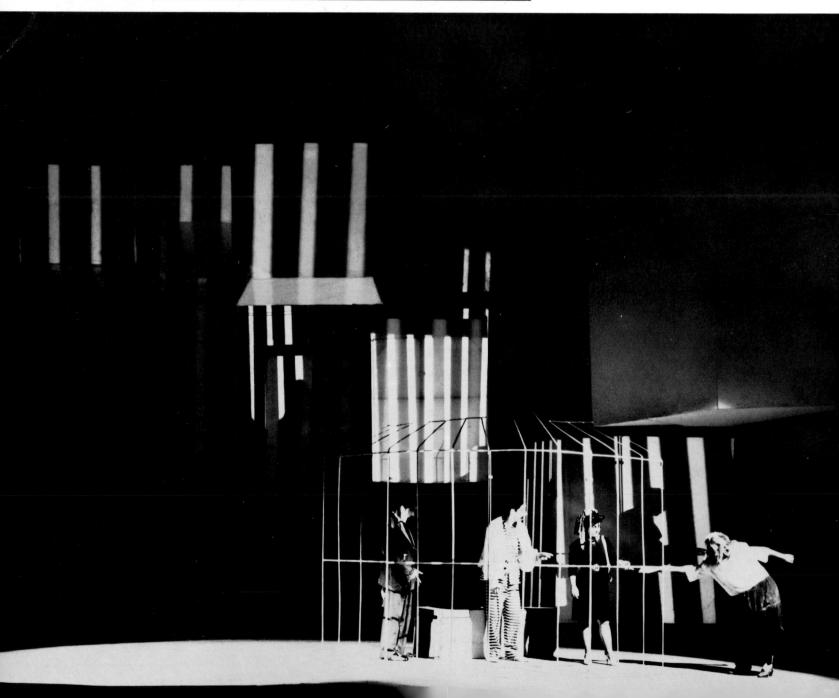

373. – FRANCOIS BILLETDOUX (1927) : *Rintru pa trou tar hin*.
1 : Yannis Kokkos. 2 : Serge Peyrat. 5 : Théâtre de la Ville.
Paris. 1970. 6 : Birgit.

374. – PETER NICHOLS (1927) : *A Day in the Death of Joe Egg*.
1 : Anne Fraser. 2 : Edgar Metcalfe. 5 : The South Australian
Theatre Company. Scott Theatre. Adelaide (Australia).
1969. 6 : Colin Ballantyne.

375. – PAVEL KOHOUT (1928) : *Cesta kolem sveta za 80 dni*.
1 : Marie Liis Kula. 2 : Voldemar Panso. 5 : Teatr Iounogo
Zritelia. Tallinn (S.S.S.R.). 1965.

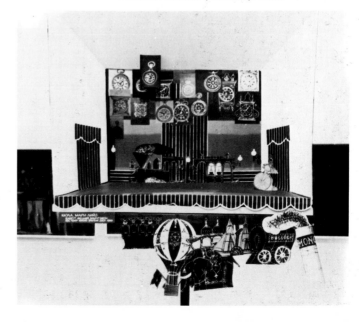

376. – EDWARD ALBEE (1928): *Tiny Alice*. **1**: Abd El Kader Farrah. **2**: Robin Phillips. **5**: Royal Shakespeare Company. Aldwych. London. 1970. **6**: Zoe Dominic. *

377. – EDWARD ALBEE (1928): *Box Mao Box*. **1**: Jörg R. Neumann – Bernd Müller. **2**: Wolfgang Lesowsky. **5**: Arena 70/71. Wiener Festwochen. Wien. 1970.

378. – DEREK WALCOTT (1930): *The Dream on Monkey Mountain*. **1**: Edward Burbridge. **2**: Michael A. Schultz. **5**: Center Theater Group of the Mark Taper Forum. Los Angeles, California (U.S.A.). 1970.

379. – SLAWOMIR MROZEK (1930): *Na Pelnym Morzu*. **1**: Marian Vanek – Milan Corba. **2**: Peter Mikulik. **5**: Divadlo na Korze. Bratislava (Ceskoslovensko). 1969.

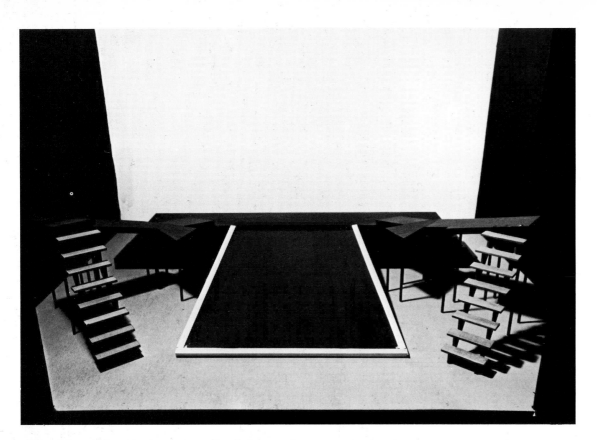

380. – YOSHIYUKI FUKUDA (1931):
Hakamadare wa dokoda. **1**: Setsu
Asakura. **2**: Hideo Kanze. **5**: Gekidan –
Seigei. Haiyûza – Gekijô. Tokyo. 1964.
6: Shigeko Higuchi.

381. – MICHAEL MCCLURE (1931): *The Beard*. **1**: Peter
H. Jurkowitsch. **2**: Götz Fritsch. **5**: Theater Creativ
im Savoy. Wien. 1969. **6**: Peter H. Jurkowitsch.

382. – HAROLD PINTER (1931) : *Landscape – Silence.*
1: John Bury. **2**: Peter Hall. **5**: Royal Shakespeare
Company. Aldwych. London. 1969. **6**: Reg Wilson. *

383. – JOSE TRIANA (1931): *La Noche de los Asesinos*. **1**: Helio Eichbauer. **2**: Martim Gonçalves. **5**: Teatro Ipanema. Rio de Janeiro (Brasil). 1969. **6**: Carlos. *

384. – JOSE TRIANA (1931): *La Noche de los Asesinos*. **1**: Christian Egemar. **2**: Anne Gullestad. **5**: Den Nationale Scene. Bergen (Norge). 1969. **6**: Trygve Schönfelder.

385/386. – JOSE TRIANA (1931): *La Noche de los Asesinos.*
1: Klaas Gubbels. **2**: John Van de Rest. **5**: Theater.
Stadsschouwburg. Nijmegen (Nederland). 1968.
6: Wouter Van Heusden.

385

386

387

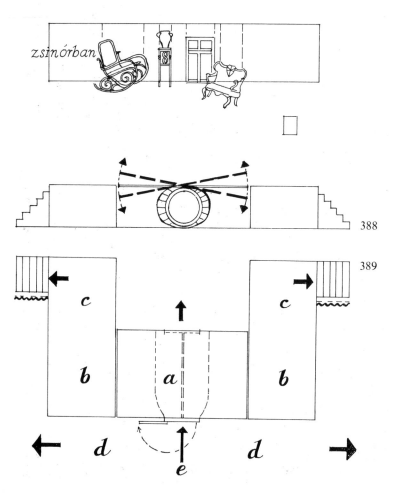

zsinórban

388

389

387/389. – ISTVAN EÖRSI (1931): *A hordok*. **1**: Gabor Szinte.
2: Istvan Horvai. **5**: Pesti Szinhaz. Budapest. 1968. *

390. – ROLF HOCHHUTH (1931): *Der Stell-vertreter*. **1**: Leo Kerz. **2**: Erwin Piscator. **5**: Freie Volksbühne. Berlin (West). 1963. **6**: Harry Croner.

391. – ROLF HOCHHUTH (1931): *Soldaten*. **1**: Wilfried Minks. **2**: Hans Schweikart. **5**: Freie Volksbühne. Berlin (West). 1967. **6**: Harry Croner.

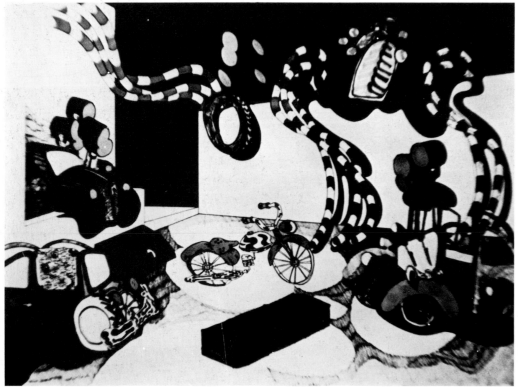

392. – FERNANDO ARRABAL (1932): *Le Jardin des Délices*. **1**: Frank Raven. **2**: Lodewijk De Boer. **3**: Louis Andriessen. **5**: Studio. De Brakke Grond. Amsterdam (Nederland). 1969. **6**: Ad Van Gessel.

393. – FERNANDO ARRABAL (1932): *Le Cimetière des Voitures*. **1**: Modesto Florez. **2**: Adolfo Gutkin. **5**: Van Troi – Oriente (Cuba). 1968. **6**: Christian Griffoul.

394/396. – FERNANDO ARRABAL
(1932) : *Le Cimetière des Voitures.*
1 : Victor Garcia. **2** : Victor Garcia.
5 : Théâtre des Arts. Paris. 1967.
6 : Bernand. *

	394
395	396

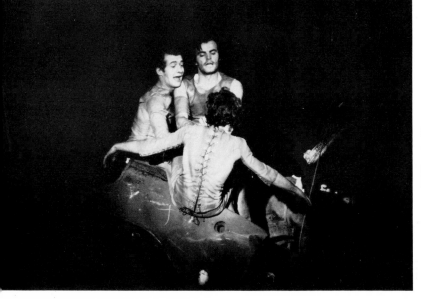

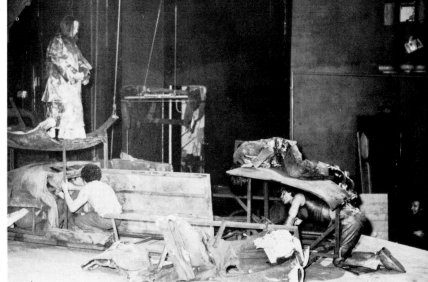

397. – BEATRICE TANAKA (1932) : *Equipée bizarre au Cirque Basile*. **1** : Béatrice Tanaka. **2** : Raphaël Gozalbo. **5** : Maison des Jeunes et de la Culture. Meudon (France). 1969.

398. – MIKHAIL CHATROV (1932) : *Bolcheviki*. **1** : Janina Malinaouskaïte. **2** : Ionas Iourachis. **5** : Dramatitcheskij Teatr. Kaunas (S.S.S.R.). 1970.

399. – LADISLAV SMOCEK (1932): *Podivné odpoledne Dr. Burkeho*. **1**: Stefan Hudak. **2**: Peter Mikulik. **5**: Mala Scéna. Bratislava (Ceskoslovensko). 1967.

400. – ANNE BARBEY (1933): *Südafrica Amen*. **1**: Jean Bosserdet. **2**: Martine Paschoud. **5**: Centre Dramatique de Lausanne – Vidy. Lausanne (Helvetia). 1971. **6**: Jacques Bétant.

401

401/402. – LeRoi Jones (1934) : *Slave Ship*. **1** : Eugene Lee.
2 : Gilbert Moses. **5** : Chelsea Theater Center, Brooklyn
Academy of Music. Brooklyn, New York (U.S.A.). 1969.
6 : Deidi Von Schaewen. *

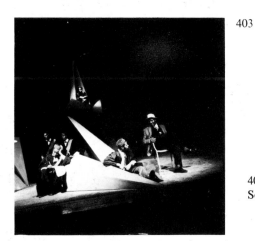

403

403. – Wole Soyinka (1934) : *Kongi's Harvest*. **1** : Wole
Soyinka. **2** : Wole Soyinka. **5** : The School of Drama
Arts Theatre. Ibadan (Nigeria). 1965.

402

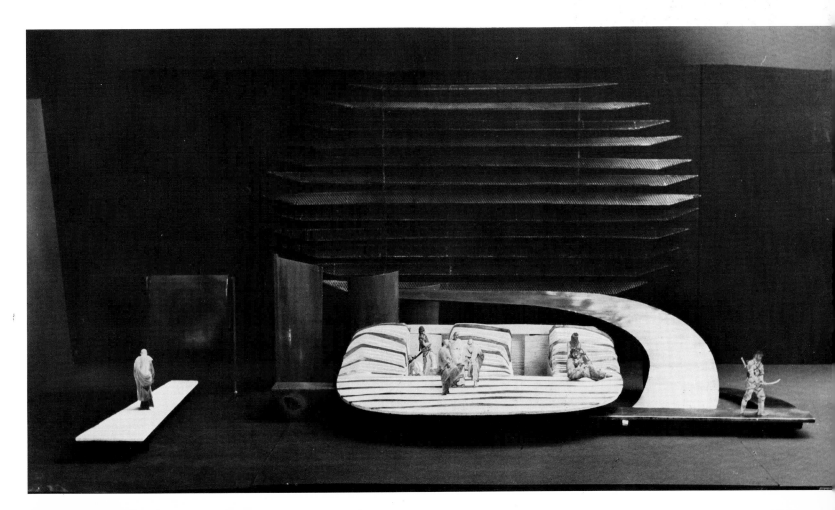

406. – DAVID LEVIN
(1935) : *Agado*
Limvugarim. **1** : Arieh
Navon. **2** : David
Levin. **3** : Frank
Pelleg. **5** : Teatron Iron
Haifa. Haifa (Israël).
1965. **6** : Keren-or.

407. – MART CROWLEY
(1935) : *The Boys in the*
Band. **1** : Peter Harvey.
2 : Robert Moore. **5** :
Richard Barr – Charles
Woodward, Jr. Theatre
Four. New York
(U.S.A.). 1968.

408. – ROCHELLE OWENS (1936): *Futz*. **1**: Richard Montgomery. **2**: Alan Robb. **5**: Creative Arts Centre. University of the West Indies (Jamaica – West Indies). 1970.

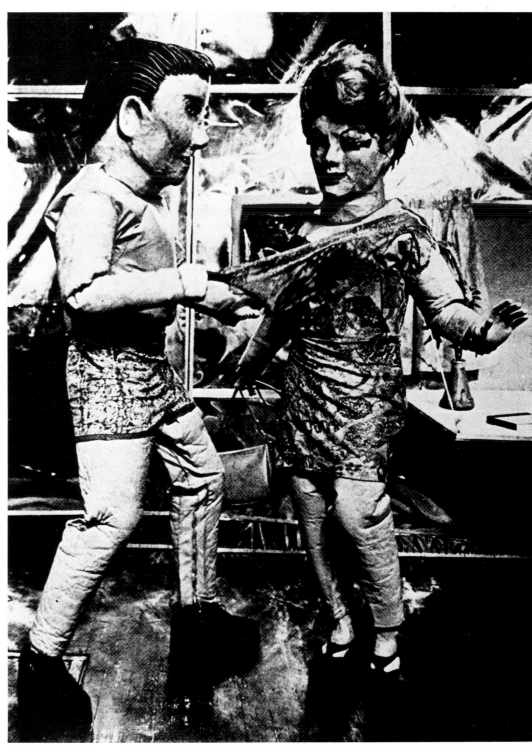

409. – JEAN-CLAUDE VAN ITALLIE (1936): *America Hurrah*. **1**: Tania Leontov. **2**: Jacques Levy – Joseph Chaikin. **3**: Marianne du Pury. **5**: Stephanie Sills Productions. Pocket Theatre. New York (U.S.A.). 1966. **6**: Bert Andrews.

410/411. – TOM STOPPARD (1937): *Rosencrantz and Guildenstern are dead*. **1**: Jürgen Rose. **2**: Hans Lietzau. **5**: Schiller Theater. Berlin (West). 1967. **6**: Ilse Buhs.

410

411

412. – TOM STOPPARD (1937): *Rosencrantz and Guildenstern are dead.* **1** : Yoshi Tosa. **2** : Robin Lovejoy. **5** : Old Tote Theatre Company. Parade Theatre. Sydney (Australia). 1969. **6** : Robert Walker.

413. – TOM STOPPARD (1937): *Rosencrantz and Guildenstern are dead.* **1** : Ary Œchslin. **2** : Gert Westphal. **5** : Stadttheater. Bern. 1968. **6** : Willi Gasché.

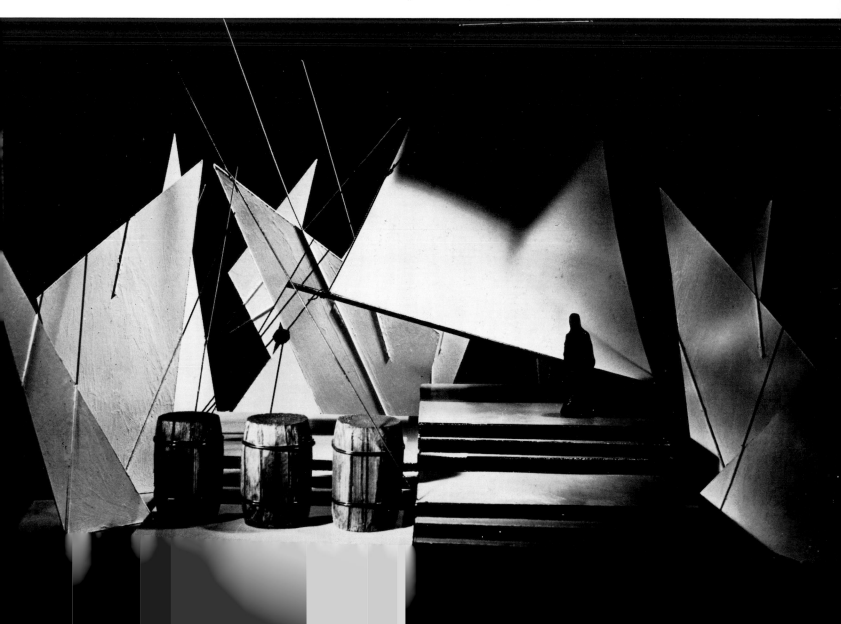

414. – FREDERIC BAAL (1940): *Real Reel.*
1 : Jean-Pol Ferbus – Frédéric Flamand.
2 : Jean-Pol Ferbus – Frédéric Flamand.
5 : Théâtre Laboratoire Vicinal.
Bruxelles. 1971. **6** : Christine Bastin.*

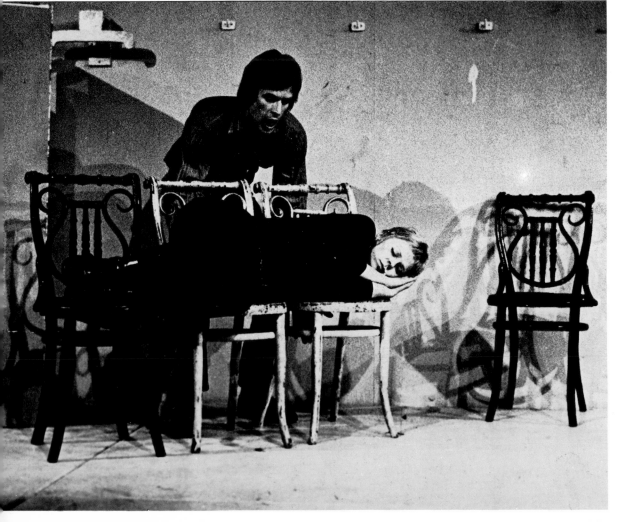

415. – HENRI KAPULAINEN (1947): *Nainen
Ystävä.* **1**: Timo Martinkauppi. **2** : Taisto-
Bertil Orsmaa. **3** : Kaj Chydenius – Tapio
Lipponen – Kim Kuusi. **5** : Ryhmä-
teatteri. Svenska Teatern. Helsinki. 1969.*

GROUPS --- GROUPES --- GRUPPEN ---
ГРУППЫ --- GRUPOS --- GRUPPI --- 集体編
GROUPS --- GROUPES --- GRUPPEN --- Г

416. – PIP SIMMONS GROUP : *Do it !* **1** : Pip Simmons Group.
2 : Pip Simmons. **3** : Chris Jordan. **4** : Eric Loeb. **5** : Arts
Lab. London. 1968. **6** : Alex Agor.

417/418. – PLAYHOUSE OF THE RIDICULOUS – TOM MURRIN:
Cock-Strong. **1**: John Vaccaro. **2**: John Vaccaro. **3**: John
Vaccaro – Ralph Czitrom. **5**: Playhouse of the Ridiculous
(New York). Théâtre 140. Bruxelles. 1971.

418

417

419

420

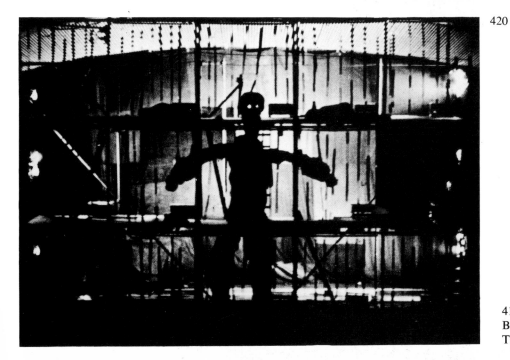

419/420. – THE LIVING THEATRE: *Frankenstein*. **1**: Julian
Beck. **2**: Judith Malina – Julian Beck. **5**: The Living
Theatre (New York). Théâtre 140. Bruxelles. 1966. *

421

421/423. – THE OTHER COMPANY: *The Pit*.
1: Naftali Yavin. **2**: Naftali Yavin. **5**: Oval.
London. 1969. **6**: Gini Robinson. *

422

423

424. – BREAD AND PUPPET THEATER:
Fire. **1**: Peter Schumann. **2**: Peter
Schumann. **5**: Bread and Puppet Theater.
New York (U.S.A.). 1966. *

425. – BREAD AND PUPPET THEATER: *The Cry of the People
for Meat*. **1**: Peter Schumann. **2**: Peter Schumann. **3**: Peter
Schumann. **5**: Bread and Puppet Theater.
New York (U.S.A.). 1969. *

426. – YOU BEIJING WEN HUA GONG ZUOZHE, GONG REN, NONG MIN, XUE SHENG JITI BIAN: *Dong Fang Hong*. **1**: You Beijing wen hua gong zuozhe, gong ren, nong min, xue sheng jiti bian. **2**: You Beijing wen hua gong zuozhe, gong ren, nong min, xue sheng jiti bian. **5**: Ba yi dianying zhipianchang, Beijingdianying zhipianchang. Beijing. 1965.

427. – ZHONGGUO WUJUTUAN JITI GAIBIAN: *Hong se niang zi jun*. **1**: Zhongguo wujutuan jiti gaibian. **2**: Zhongguo wujutuan jiti gaibian. **5**: Zhongguo wujutuan yanchu. Beijingdianying zhipianchang. Beijing. 1970.

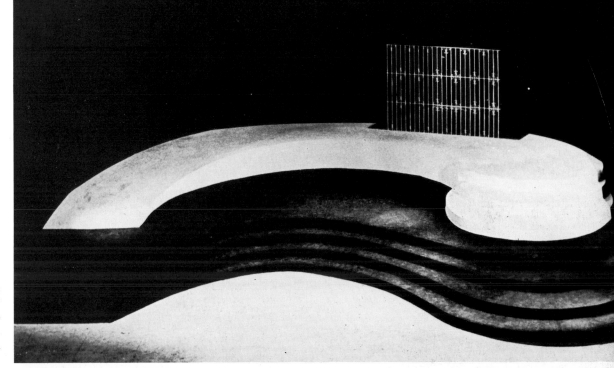

428. – CLAUDIO MONTEVERDI (1567-1643):
Lacrime d'Amante al Sepolcro dell'
Amata. **1**: Sarah Feres. **2**: Marbo
Giannaccini. **4**: Marbo Giannaccini.
5: Teatro da Paz. Belém do Para
(Brasil). 1966. **6**: Oscar Ramos.

429. – ANTONIO VIVALDI (1678-1741):
Le Quattro Stagioni. **1**: Bernard Schultze
– Pet Halmen. **4**: Erich Walter. **5**:
Deutsche Oper am Rhein. Düsseldorf –
Duisburg (BRD). 1967. **6**: Rudolf Ejmke.

430. – WOLFGANG AMADEUS MOZART (1756-1791): *Cosi fan Tutte*. **1**: Camillo Osorovitz. **2**: Jacques Luccioni. **5**: Centre Populaire Lyrique de France. Théâtre Gérard Philipe. Saint-Denis (France). 1967. **6**: Jacques Citles.

431. – BEETHOVEN (1770-1827): *Fidelio*. **1**: Allan Lees. **2**: John Copley. **5**: The Australian Opera. Her Majesty's Theatre. Sydney (Australia). 1970.

432	433
	434
	435
	436
	437

432/437. – GIOACCHINO ROSSINI (1792-1868): *Il Barbiere di Siviglia*. **1**: Achim Freyer. **2**: Ruth Berghaus. **5**: Deutsche Staatsoper. Berlin D.D.R. 1968. **6**: Marion Schöne.

438. – HECTOR BERLIOZ (1803-1869) : *Les Troyens*. **1** : Nicholas Georgiadis. **2** : Minos Volanakis. **5** : Royal Opera House. London. 1969. **6** : Zoe Dominic.

440. – RICHARD WAGNER (1813-1883) : *Tannhäuser*. **1** : Wieland Wagner. **2** : Wieland Wagner. **4** : Festspielhaus. Bayreuth (BRD). 1964. **6** : Siegfried Lauterwasser.

439. – HECTOR BERLIOZ (1803-1869) : *Les Troyens*. **1** : Nicholas Georgiadis. **2** : Minos Volanakis. **5** : Royal Opera House. London. 1969. **6** : Donald Southern.

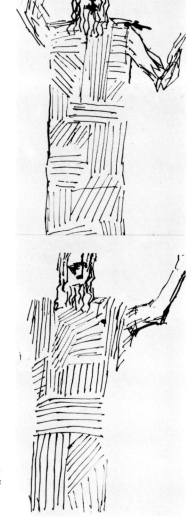

441. – RICHARD WAGNER (1813-1883): *Der Ring des Nibelungen.* **1**: Anne-Marie Simond – Pierre Simond. **5**: Lausanne (Helvetia). 1969. **6**: Claude Huber.

442. – RICHARD WAGNER (1813-1883): *Das Rheingold.* **1**: Fritz Wotruba. **2**: Gustav Rudolf Sellner. **5**: Deutsche Oper. Berlin (West). 1967. **6**: Vilém Sochurek.

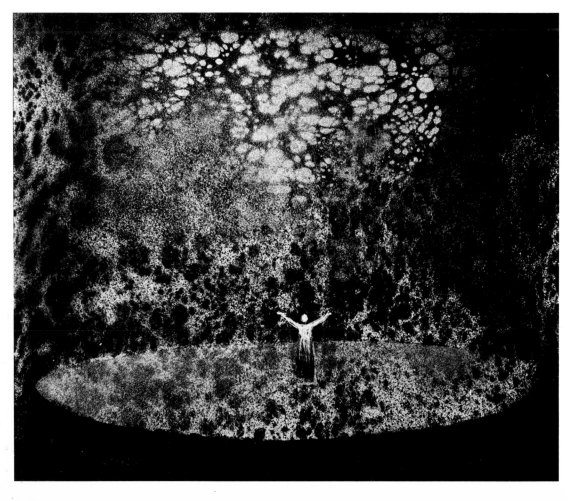

443. – RICHARD WAGNER (1813-1883): *Siegfried.* **1**: Jan Brazda. **2**: Folke Abenius. **5**: Kungliga Teatern Operan. Stockholm. 1970. **6**: Enar-Merkel Ryberg.

444. – GIUSEPPE VERDI (1813-1901): *Macbeth.* **1**: Rudolf
Heinrich **2**: Otto Schenk. **5**: Bayerische Staatsoper.
München (BRD). 1967. **6**: Sabine Toepffer.

445. – GIUSEPPE VERDI (1813-1901): *Macbeth.*
1: Rudolf Heinrich. **2**: Otto Schenk. **5**: Bayerische
Staatsoper. München (BRD). 1967.
6: Rudolf Betz.

446. – GIUSEPPE VERDI (1813-
1901): *Aida*. **1**: Wieland
Wagner. **2**: Wieland Wagner.
5: Deutsche Oper. Berlin
(West). 1962. **6**: Ilse Buhs.

447/448. – GIUSEPPE VERDI
(1813-1901): *Il Trovatore*. **1**:
Mikulas Kravjansky.
2: Vladislav Hamsik. **5**:
Statne Divadlo Ostrava.
Ostrava (Ceskoslovensko).
1966.

449. – GEORGES BIZET
(1838-1875): *Carmen*.
1: Vittorio Gregotti –
Giosetta Fioroni – **2**:
Alberto Arbasino.
4: Carlo Faraboni. **5**:
Teatro Comunale.
Bologna. (Italia). 1967.

451. – GEORGES BIZET (1838-1875) – ROMAN SHTCHEDRINE : ▶
Carmen. **1**: Boris Messerer. **4**: Alberto Alonso.
5: Bolshoj Teatr. Moskva. 1967.

450. – GEORGES BIZET (1838-1875) :*Carmen*. **1**: Marina
Sokolova. **2**: Walter Felsenstein. **5**: Mouzykalnyj Teatr
imeni Stanislavskogo i Nemirovitcha – Dantchenko.
Moskva. 1969. **6**: Christian Griffoul.

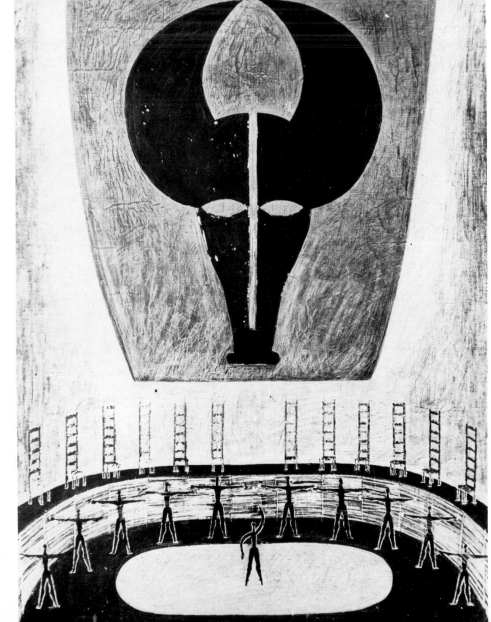

452. – MODEST MOUSSORGSKIJ (1839-1881): *Boris Godounov.*
1: Nikolaj Zolotarev. 2: Lev Mikhailov. 5: Teatr Opery i
Baleta. Tbilissi (S.S.S.R.). 1966. 6: Vilém Sochurek.

453. – MODEST MOUSSORGSKIJ (1839-1881): *Boris Godounov.*
1: Miomir Denic. 2: Mladen Sabljic. 5: Opera Narodnog
pozorista. Beograd. 1962. 6: Miroslav Krstic.

454. – MODEST MOUSSORGSKIJ (1839-1881): *Khovanshtchina.*
1: Valerij Levental. 2: Boris Pokrovskij. 5: Bolgarskaja
Narodnaja Opera. Sofia. 1966.

455. – LEOS JANACEK (1854-1928): *Jeji pastorkyna*. **1**: Reinhart Zimmermann – Jan Skalicky. **2**: Götz Friedrich. **5**: Komische Oper. Berlin D.D.R. 1964. **6**: Arwid Lagenpusch.

456. – PIETRO MASCAGNI (1863-1945): *Cavalleria Rusticana*. **1**: Luciano Damiani. **2**: Giorgio Strehler. **5**: Teatro alla Scala. Milano (Italia). 1966. **6**: E. Piccagliani.

457. – RICHARD
STRAUSS (1864-
1949) : *Die Frau
ohne Schatten*. **1** :
Josef Svoboda.
2 : Rudolf Hart-
mann. **5** : Royal
Opera House.
Covent Garden.
London. 1967.

458. – ALEXANDR
SKRIABIN (1872-
1915) : *P o e m a
Extaza*. **1** : Jürgen
Rose. **4** : John
C r a n k o. **5** :
Württembergische
S t a a t s t h e a t e r.
Stuttgart (BRD).
1962.

459. – ARNOLD SCHÖNBERG (1874-1951): *Moses und Aron.*
1: Heinrich Wendel. **2**: Georg Reinhardt. **4**: Erich Walter.
5: Deutsche Oper am Rhein. Düsseldorf-Duisburg (BRD).
1968. **6**: Elfi Hess. *

460. – ARNOLD SCHÖNBERG (1874-1951): *Die Jacobsleiter.*
1: Neil Peter Jampolis – Hal George. **2**: Bodo Igesz.
5: Sante Fe Opera. Opera Theatre. Sante Fe, New Mexico
(U.S.A.). 1968. *

461. – MAURICE RAVEL (1875-1937) : *Boléro*. **1** : Minas Avetissian. **2** : Azat Garibian. **5** : Teatr Opery i Baleta. Erevan (S.S.S.R.). 1966.

462. – BELA BARTOK (1881-1945) : *A csodalatos mandarin*. **1** :Bernard Daydé. **4** : Joseph Lazzini. **5** : O.R.T.F. Paris. 1967. **6** : Serge Lido.

463. – IGOR STRAVINSKIJ (1882-1971):
L'Oiseau de Feu. **1**: Jürgen Rose.
4: John Cranko. **5**: Deutsche Oper.
Berlin (West). 1964. **6**: Harry Croner.

464. – IGOR STRAVINSKIJ (1882-1971):
Mavra. **1**: Eugenio Guglielminetti.
2: Aldo Trionfo. **4**: Mario Pistoni.
5: Teatro Comunale. Bologna (Italia).
1970.

465. – IGOR STRAVINSKIJ (1882-1971): *Œdipus Rex*. **1**: John Ezell. **2**: Ronald Mitchell. **3**: Jean Cocteau – Jean Danielou. **5**: Wisconsin Union Theatre, University of Wisconsin. Madison, Wisconsin (U.S.A.). 1968.
6: Duane Hopp. *

466. – IGOR STRAVINSKIJ (1882-1971): *Œdipus Rex*. **1**: Dusan Ristic. **2**: Ani Radosevic. **5**: Opera Narodnog pozorista. Beograd. 1967.
6: Miroslav Krstic.

467

468

469

467/469. – ALBAN BERG (1885-1935): *Wozzeck*. **1**: Ugo
Mulas – Virginio Puecher – Ebe Colciaghi. **2**: Virginio
Puecher. **3**: Georg Büchner – Alberto Mantelli. **5**: Teatro
Comunale. Bologna (Italia). 1969.

470

471

472

470/472. – ALBAN BERG (1885-1935): *Lulu*. **1**: Thierry Vernet. **2**: Lotfi Mansouri. **5**: Grand Théâtre de Genève. Genève (Helvetia). 1971.

473. – JACQUES IBERT (1890-1962): *Le Roi d'Yvetot*. **1**: Jacques Carelman. **2**: Bronislav Horowicz. **3**: Jacques Limozin – André de la Tourasse. **5**: Opéra de Strasbourg. Strasbourg (France). 1961. **6**: Jacques Carelman.

474. – SERGHEJ PROKOFIEV (1891-1953): *Romeo i Djioulietta*. **1**: Valerij Levental. **4**: Oleg Vinogradov. **5**: Teatr Opery i Baleta. Novossibirsk (S.S.S.R.). 1964.

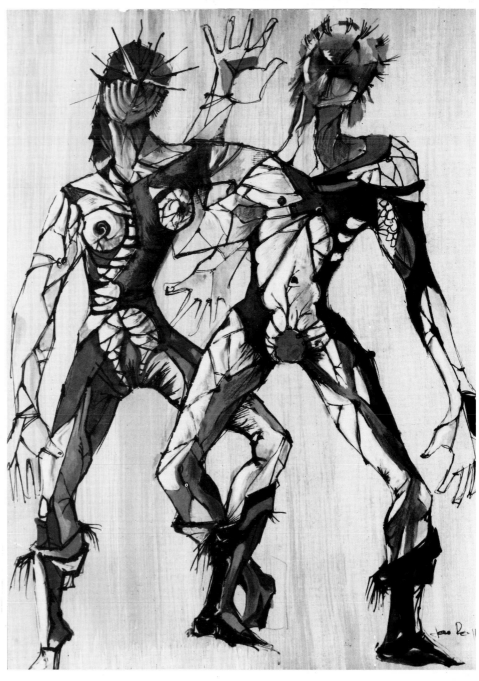

475. – SERGHEJ PROKOFIEV (1891-1953): *Skifskaïa Siouita* (*Ala i Lollij*). **1**: Jacques Rapp. **4**: Victorio Biaggi. **5**: Théâtre de l'Opéra. Lyon (France). 1970.

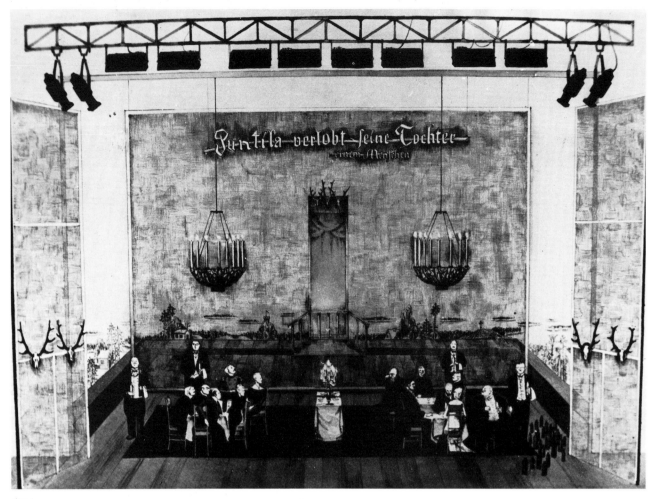

476

476/479. – PAUL DESSAU (1894): *Herr Puntila und sein Knecht Matti*. **1**: Andreas Reinhardt. **2**: Ruth Berghaus. **3**: Bertolt Brecht. **5**: Deutsche Staatsoper. Berlin D.D.R. 1966. **6**: Vilém Sochurek.

477

478 479

480

481

480/482. – PAUL HINDEMITH (1895-1964): *Hérodiade*.
1 : Peter Docherty. **2** : Vincent Guy. **3** : Stéphane Mallarmé.
4 : Peter Darrell. **5** : Scottish Theatre Ballet. London. 1970.
6 : Anthony Crickmay.

482

483. – CARL ORFF (1895):
Die Kluge. **1**: Lawrence
Schafer. **2** : Herman
Geiger – Torel. **5** : Royal
Conservatory of Music
Opera School. Toronto
(Canada). 1966.

484. – CARL ORFF (1895):
Prometheus. **1** : Josef
S v o b o d a. **2** : August
Everding. **5** : Bayerische
S t a a t s o p e r. München
(BRD). 1968. *

485. – KURT WEILL (1900-1950): *Aufstieg und Fall der Stadt Mahagonny*. **1**: Ralph Koltai. **2**: Michael Geliot. **3**: Bertolt Brecht. **5**: Sadlers Wells Opera. London. 1963. **6**: Alexander Low. *

486. – KURT WEILL (1900-1950): *Aufstieg und Fall der Stadt Mahagonny*. **1**: Jacques Rapp. **2**: Louis Erlo. **3**: Bertolt Brecht. **5**: Opéra de Lyon. Lyon (France). 1970.

487. – BORIS BLACHER (1903):
Zwischenfälle bei einer Notlandung.
1: Max Bill. **2**: Gustav Rudolf
Sellner. **3**: Heinz Von Cramer.
4: Deryk Mendel. **5**:
Hamburgische Staatsoper.
Hamburg (BRD). 1966. **6**: Peyer.

488

489

488/489. – LUIGI DALLAPICCOLA (1904):
Ulisse. **1**: Heinrich Wendel. **2**:
Georg Reinhardt. **5**: Deutsche Oper
am Rhein. Düsseldorf-Duisburg.
(BRD). 1970. **6**: Rudolf Eimke.

. – MICHAEL
PETT (1905):
g Priam. **1**: Sean
nny. **2**: Sam
namaker. **5**:
oyal Opera
use. London.
2. **6**: Houston
Rogers.

. – MICHAEL
PETT (1905): *The
t Garden.* **1**:
nothy O'Brien.
Peter Hall. **5**:
oyal Opera
use. London.
0. **6**: Stuart
Robinson.

492. – MAURICE THIRIET (1906):
Œdipe-Roi. **1**: Yves-Bonnat. **2**:
Louis Erlo. **3**: Jean Cocteau. **5**:
Festival de Lyon. Théâtre Romain.
Lyon (France). 1962. **6**: H.U.
Schlumpf.

494. – GIAN CARLO MENOTTI (1911): ▶
The Telephone. **1**: Frans Vossen.
2: Frans Boerlage. **5**: Opera Studio
van de Nederlandse Opera Stichting.
Kleine Komedie. Amsterdam
(Nederland). 1969. **6**: Maria Austria.

493. – DIMITRIJ SHOSTAKOVITCH
(1906): *Katerina Izmaïlova*. **1**: David
Borovskij. **2**: Molossova –
Klementiev. **5**: Teatr Opery i Baleta.
Chevtchenko (S.S.S.R.). 1965.

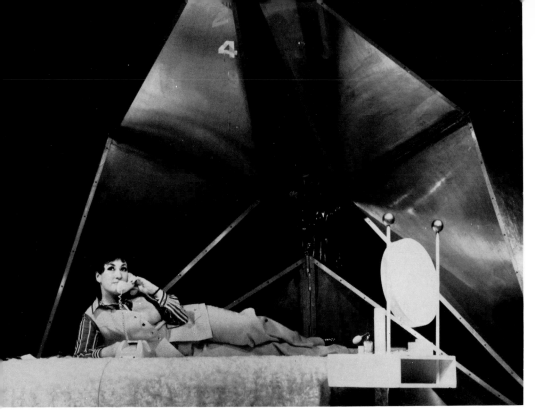
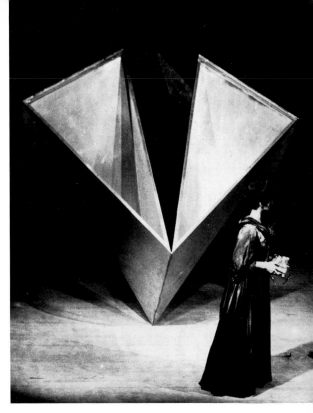

495. – BENJAMIN BRITTEN (1913) –
HENRY PURCELL – IMOGEN HOLST :
Dido and Aeneas. **1** : Frans Vossen.
2 : Frans Boerlage. **3** : Nahum Tate –
Vergilius. **5** : Opera Studio van de
Nederlandse Opera Stichting. Kleine
Komedie. Amsterdam (Nederland).
1969. **6** : Maria Austria.

496/497. – WITOLD LUTOSLAWSKI (1913) :
3 *Poèmes d'Henri Michaux*. **1** : André
Acquart. **4** : Milko Sparemblek. **5** :
Fondation Gulbenkian. Lisboa. 1970.

496
497

498. – MORDECHAI SETTER (1916) : *Nashim Ba'Ohel.* **1** : Dani
Karavan. **2** : Rena Gluck. **5** : Lahakat Machol Bat Sheva.
Tel-Aviv. 1966. **6** : Jaacov Agor. *

499

499/500. – MORDECHAI SETTER (1916) : *Part Real Part Dream.*
1 : Dani Karavan. **4** : Martha Graham. **5** : Martha Graham
Dance Company. New York (U.S.A.). 1965. **6** : Jaacov Agor.

500

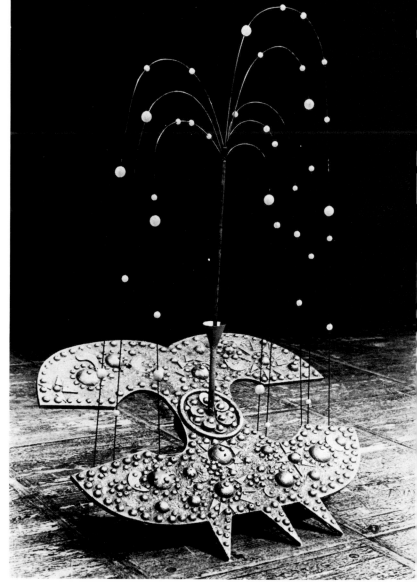

501. – YVAN SEMENOFF (1917): *Don Juan ou L'Amour de la Géométrie.* **1** : Isabelle Echari – Diego Etcheverry. **2** : Jacques Luccioni. **3** : Max Frisch. **5** : Centre Lyrique Populaire de France. Théâtre Gérard Philipe. Saint-Denis (France). 1969. **6** : Claude Poirier.

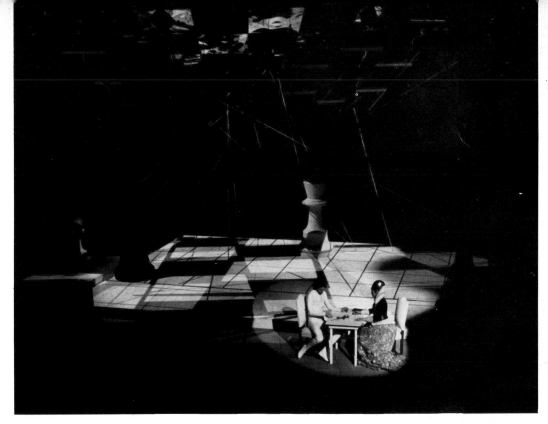

502. – KARA KARAEV (1918) : *Teni nad Kobistanom.* **1** : Togroul Narimanbekov. **4** : Maksoud Makmedov – Rafiga Akhoundova. **5** : Teatr Opery i Baleta imeni M. Akhoundova. Bakou (S.S.R.). 1968.

503/504. – BERND ALOIS ZIMMERMANN (1918-1970): *Die Soldaten*. **1**: Heinrich Wendel. **2**: Georg Reinhardt. **5**: Deutsche Oper am Rhein. Düsseldorf-Duisburg (BRD). 1971. **6**: Fred Kliché.

505

506

507

505/507. – BERND ALOIS ZIMMERMANN (1918-1970): *Die Soldaten*. **1** : Josef Svoboda. **2** : Vaclav Kaslik. **5** : Bayerische Staatsoper. München (BRD). 1969. *

508

508/510. – ROMAN HAUBENSTOCK – RAMATI (1919) : *Amerika.*
1 : Michel Raffaëlli. **2** : Deryk Mendel. **3** : Franz Kafka.
5 : Deutsche Oper. Berlin (West). 1966. **6** : Ilse Buhs.

510

509

511. – GINO NEGRI (1919): *Giovanni Sebastiano*. **1**: Eugenio Guglielminetti. **2**: Aldo Trionfo. **4**: Mario Pistoni. **5**: Teatro Comunale. Bologna (Italia). 1970. **6**: Claudio Strudthoff.

512. – LUIGI NONO (1924): *La Fabbrica illuminata*. **1**: Antonello Madau Diaz. **2**: Antonello Madau Diaz. **3**: Giuliano Scabia – Cesare Pavese. **4**: Luciana Novaro. **5**: Teatro Comunale. Bologna (Italia). 1971.

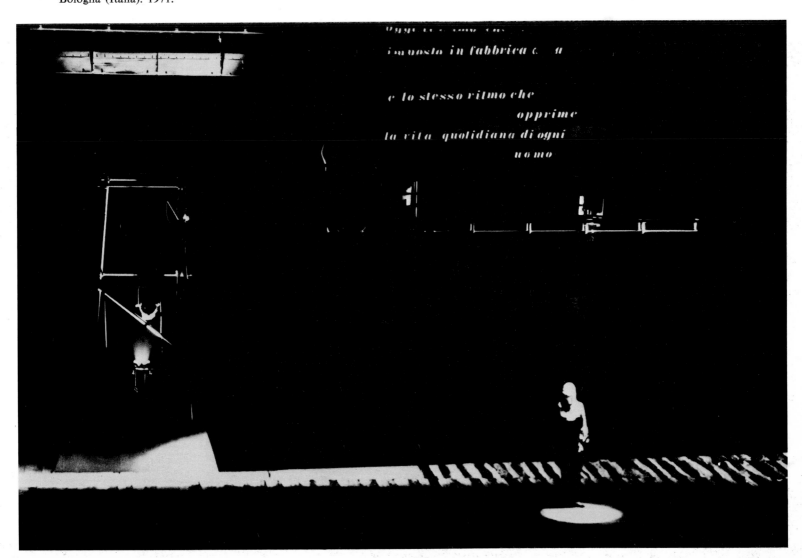

513

514

513/515. — LUIGI NONO (1924): *Intolleranza*. **1**: Josef Svoboda. **2**: S. Caldwell. **5**: The Opera Group of Boston. Boston (U.S.A.). 1965. **6**: Miroslav Pflug. *

515

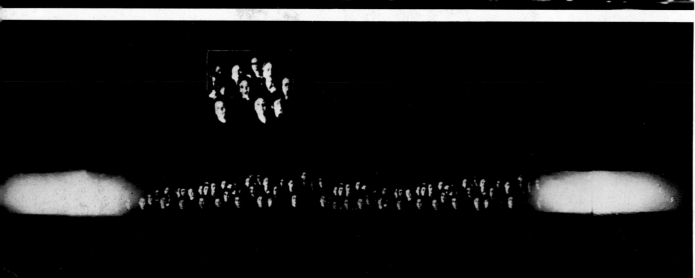

516

517

516/518. – HARRY SOMERS (1925): *Louis Riel*. **1**: Murray
Laufer – Marie Day. **2**: Leon Major. **3**: Mavor Moore.
5: Canadian Opera Company. O'Keefe Centre.
Toronto (Canada). 1967.

518

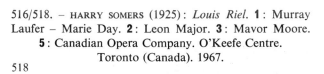

519. – LUCIANO BERIO (1925): *Allez-Hop !*
1: Emanuele Luzzati. **2**: Luciano Berio.
3: Italo Calvino. **4**: Marise Flach. **5**: Teatro
Comunale. Bologna (Italia). 1968.

520. – HANS WERNER HENZE (1926): *Der junge
Lord.* **1**: Reinhart Zimmermann – Eleonore
Kleiber. **2**: Joachim Herz. **3**: Ingeborg
Bachmann. **4**: Tom Schilling. **5**: Komische
Oper. Berlin D.D.R. 1968.
6: Arwid Lagenpusch.

521. – JEAN PRODROMIDES (1927): *Une Saison en Enfer*. **1**: Bernard Daydé. **3**: Arthur Rimbaud – Joanne Klein. **4**: Joseph Lazzini. **5**: Théâtre Français de la Danse. Théâtre de l'Odéon. Paris. 1969. **6**: Pic.

522. – MAURICE BEJART (1927): *Baudelaire*. **1**: Roger Bernard – Joëlle Roustan. **3**: Charles Baudelaire – Maurice Béjart. **4**: Maurice Béjart. **5**: Ballet du XXème siècle. Cirque Royal. Bruxelles. 1968.

523. – VITTORIO FELLEGARA (1927) : *Mutazioni*. **1** : Achille Perilli. **4** : Mario Pistoni. **5** : Teatro alla Scala. Milano (Italia). 1965. **6** : E. Piccagliani.

524. – STEPHEN SONDHEIM (1930) : *Company*. **1** : Boris Aronson. **2** : Harold Prince. **3** : George Furth. **4** : Michael Bennett. **5** : Harold Prince – Ruth Mitchell. Alvin Theatre. New York (U.S.A.). 1970. **6** : Robert Galbraith.

525. – GALT MACDERMOT (1930): *Hair*. **1**: Ming Cho Lee.
2: Gerald Freedman. **3**: Gerome Ragni – James Rado.
    5: New York Shakespeare Festival Public Theater.
            New York (U.S.A.). 1967.

526. – TAKU IZUMI (1930): *Sayonara Tyo!* **1**: Kaoru Kanamori. **2**: Keita Asari. **3**: Hiroo Sakata. **5**: Gekidan – Shiki. Nissei Gekijô. Tokyo. 1970.

527. – SERGHEJ SLONIMSKIJ (1932): *Virineia.* **1**: Nikolaj Zolotarev. **2**: Lev Mikhailov. **5**: Mouzykalnyj Teatr imeni Stanislavskogo i Nemirovitcha – Dantchenko. Moskva. 1967.

528 | 529
—————
| 530
—————
531
—————
| 532

528/532. – GIACOMO MANZONI (1932): *Atomtod*. **1**: Josef
Svoboda. **2**: Virginio Puecher. **5**: Piccola Scala.
Milano (Italia). 1965. **6**: E. Piccagliani. *

533

534

533/534. – PETER SCHAT (1935) : *Labirint*. **1** : Aldo Van Eyck
2 : Peter Oosthoek. **3** : Lodewijk De Boer. **4** : Koert Stuyf
5 : Nederlandse Opera Stichting en het Holland Festival.
Carré. Amsterdam (Nederland). 1966. **6** : Maria Austria

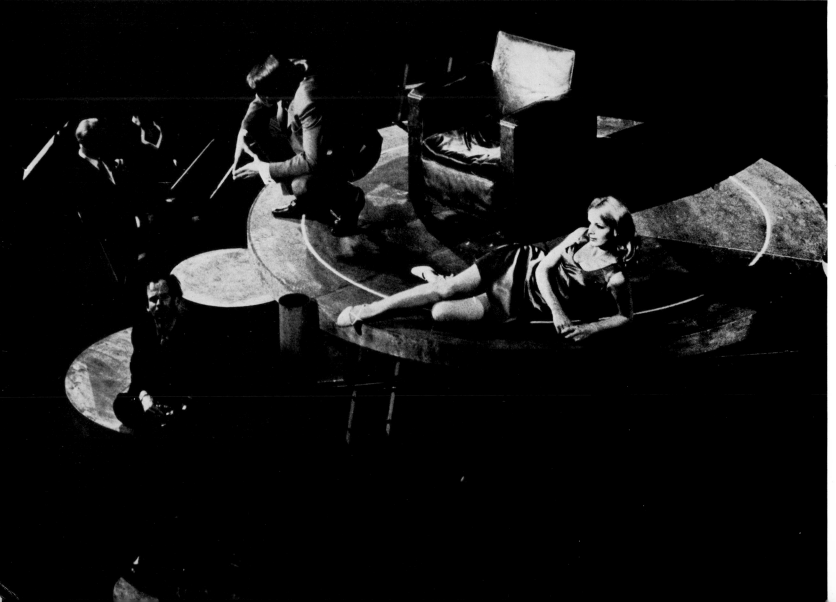

ANALOGIES OF STYLES AND OF TECHNIQUES

The illustrations in this book provide the opportunity of comparing settings of diverse origins bearing on the same work. To be comprehensive, we would have liked to outline some analogies of styles resulting from the choice of identical techniques.
The following illustrations thus constitute examples of:

> the utilization of mirrors (ill. 535, 536, 537; see also ill. 163-165, 382, 521),
> the utilization of photographic or cinematographic projections and of photographic collages (ill. 538, 539, 540; see also ill. 85, 256, 273, 290, 308, 322, 324, 362, 371, 400, 467-469, 485, 503-504, 505-507, 513-515, 516-518),
> the resurgence—stemming from the popular traditions—of the use of masks, of mask-costumes, of puppets, of puppets disguising actors, of puppets forming the setting and of giant dolls (ill. 541, 542, 543, 544, 545, 546, 547, 548, 549, 550, 551; see also ill. 19-30, 41, 257, 278, 408, 409, 424, 425, 480-482).

The reader will find, in the first part of the illustrations, analogies between techniques. Such, for instance, as the fairly wide-spread tendency to disembody, to perforate the architectural elements, so that only the suggestive impact of their skeletons remains.

Starting with naked tubular construction, this process culminates in monumental sculpture all pierced with holes, textile fabrics reduced to shreds, or else in structures built of old and often half-burnt planks (see ill. 31, 73, 84, 89, 97-100, 122, 287, 444-445).

In such cases, the elements called rostrums are frequently devoid of any kind of decorative feature, their structure being self-sufficient (see ill. 4, 79-83, 246).

And one thus attains, by a logical process of suppression of non-essentials, the notion of open or enclosed "free space", which calls totally in question the former configurations of the places of performance (see ill. 1, 14-17, 35-39, 43-45, 54-47, 93, 101, 232-233, 354-358, 368-369, 401-402, 421-423).

YVES-BONNAT

I. MIRRORS

At the far end of a setting which extends the architectural structure and style of the auditorium, a mirror reproduces the acting in reverse.

535. — SAMUEL BECKETT: *En attendant Godot.* **1**: Josef Svoboda. **2**: Otomar Krejca. **5**: Salzburger Festspiele. Landestheater. Salzburg (Österreich). 1970.

537. — JEAN RACINE: *Bérénice.* **1**: René Allio. **2**: Roger Planchon. **5**: Théâtre de la Cité. Villeurbanne (France). 1969.
6: Nicolas Treatt.

The combination of several mirrors not only multiplies the aspects and the dimensions of the setting, but also creates a sumptuous aesthetic vision.

536. — TIBOR DERY: *A tükör.* **1**: Lajos Janosa. **2**: Dezso Kapas. **5**: Vigszinhaz. Budapest. 1969.

The recourse to aluminium panels operating as mirrors is justified by the title of the work, which intermingles two simultaneous actions located in two rooms placed one within the other. The mirrors reflect the setting and the acting, as well as certain violent lighting effects at the end of the play.

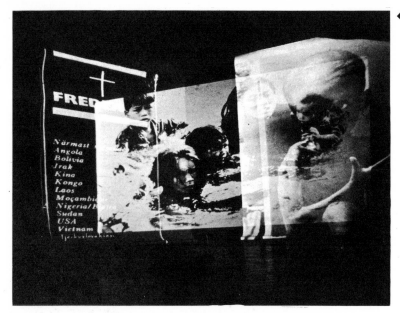

Superimpositions of projections of documentary and other images.

◀ **538.** – E E V A - L I I S A MANNER – ROLF EDBERG – WISLAWA SZYMBORSKA : *Strontium.* **1** : Lars-Henrik Schönberg. **2** : Katri Nironen. **5** : Collegium Artium. Helsinki. 1968. **6** : Lars-Henrik Schönberg.

541. – SOPHOCLES – JOHN ▶ LEWIN : *Oidipous Tyrannos.* **1** : Yoshi Tosa. **2** : Tyrone Guthrie. **5** : Old Tote Theatre Company. Clancy Auditorium, University of New South Wales. Sydney (Australia). 1970. **6** : Barry Michael.

Dehumanization of the actors: their masks, the ornaments of their costumes and their gloves make some look like statues, others like insects.

On suspended mobile panels are stuck photos of the instruments composing the musical score of the ballet. The appearance of each photo coincides with the entrance of the instrument it represents.

◀ **539.** – DAVE BRUBEK : *Jazz-out.* **1** : Yves-Bonnat. **4** : Françoise Dupuy – Dominique Dupuy. **5** : Théâtre de l'Opéra. Mulhouse (France). 1966. **6** : J.P. Schwartz.

540. – ARMAND GATTI : *V comme Vietnam.* **1** : Manfred Grund. **2** : Hans-Joachim Martens – Wolfgang Pintzka. **5** : Volksbühne. Berlin D.D.R. 1969. **6** : Harry Hirschfeld.

542. – ALFRED JARRY : *Ubu Roi.* **1** : Franciszka Themerson. **2** : Michael Meschke. **3** : Krzysztof Penderecki. **5** : Marionetteatern. Stockholm. 1968. **6** : Beata Bergström.

Projections simulating the reception of television broadcasts.

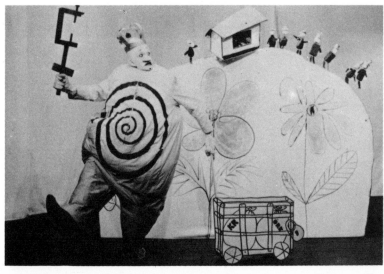

Combination of the technique of the mask and that of the puppet. Thanks to his disguise and gestures, the live actor is able to assume the aspect of the puppets moving around at the top of the setting.

Masks have enabled the scene designer to impart life to the drawings with which Jarry illustrated his play.

543. – ALFRED JARRY – JEAN-LOUIS BARRAULT : *Jarry sur la Butte*. **1** : Jacques Noël. **2** : Jean-Louis Barrault. **3** : Michel Legrand. **4** : Norbert Schmucki. **5** : Elysée – Montmartre. Paris. 1970. **6** : Bernand.

546. – VLADIMIR MAIAKOVSKIJ : *Bania*. **1** : Jozef Szajna. **2** : Jozef Szajna. **5** : Stary Teatr. Krakow (Polska). 1967. **6** : Wojciech Plewinski.

Adoption of the system employed for the traditional "giants" of popular pageants. The bearer, concealed beneath the figure's garments, forms an integral part of the giant and is thus able to ensure both its progress and its gestures.

Use of actors disproportionately disguised as puppets in an action involving human characters.

◀ 544. – BOGDAN CIPLIC : *Slatko pravoslavlje*. **1** : Dusan Ristic. **2** : Dimitrije Djurkovic. **5** : Atelje 212. Beograd. 1970. **6** : Branko Cugelj.

547. – ROGER PLANCHON : *Bleus, blancs, rouges*. **1** : André Acquart – Claude Acquart. **2** : Roger Planchon. **3** : Claude Lochy. **5** : Théâtre de la Cité. Villeurbanne (France). 1971.

The puppets assume the shape of banners, which serve diversely as properties, settings, symbols or characters.

Utilization of an old fair-ground technique: the puppet with a human face—that of the puppeteer himself, whose hands, concealed behind the fence and in the body of the marionette, animate the latter in a burlesque manner.

◀ 545. – PETER WEISS : *Die Verfolgung und Ermordung Jean Paul Marats, dargestellt durch die Schauspielgruppe des Hospizes zu Charenton, unter Anleitung des Hernn de Sade*. **1** : Francisco Nieva. **2** : Adolfo Marsillach. **5** : Teatro Español. Madrid. 1968.

This enormous head represents a monster. To insure total stability it has been fashioned in the shape of a tent of which the support is a variable-volume umbrella worked by three people. The latter open and close «windows» in the covering and, by passing their hands and heads through them, modify the head of the monster and, consequently, its expression; they also lend it speech by means of a megaphone. At the beginning and end of the performance, the monster is folded flat on the stage-floor and is, therefore, invisible.

548. – PETER WEISS: *Gesang vom lusitanischen Popanz.*
1: Ilona Keserü. **2**: Tamas Major. **5**: Katona Jozsef Szinhaz. Budapest. 1970.

A mime-dancer embodying Diaghilev leads by the hand a giant puppet representing the same character in a caricatural manner; Diaghilev's arm is extensible.

549. – PIP SIMMONS GROUP: *Do it !* **1**: Pip Simmons Group. **2**: Pip Simmons. **4**: Eric Loeb. **5**: Arts Lab. London. 1968. **6**: Roger Perry.

550/551. – MAURICE BEJART – PIERRE HENRY: *Nijinsky, Clown de Dieu.*
1: Roger Bernard – Joëlle Roustan. **4**: Maurice Béjart. **5**: Ballet du XXème siècle. Cirque Royal. Bruxelles. 1971. **6**: Christian Gibey.

Parade of characters whose over-sized, carnival-like heads evoke the various ranks of society: military men, magistrates, members of the middle-class, financiers, proletarians, clerics, etc...

Giant carnival masks with caricatural and satirical intent.

WORKING NOTES

The photo of a setting conveys a very imperfect idea of its function and utilization. When we sent out a call for iconographic documents, we consequently asked that these should be accompanied by technical notes, original or already published, explaining the purpose served by the scenography and the manner in which it operates.

Lack of space prevents the publication of all the notes received: only those which we regard as strictly indispensable have been retained.

The number placed before each note refers to the illustrations concerned.

René Hainaux - Christiane Fraipont

1. AESCHYLUS: Oresteia (The Oresteia).

The performance takes place on three consecutive evenings. The production is conceived for open spaces: gymnasia, school-rooms, workshops, churches, barrack-yards and the like.

3. AESCHYLUS - HUBERT GIGNOUX: La Prise de l'Orestie (The Capture of the Oresteia).

Neither a translation nor an adaptation, but a free critical interpretation of Aeschylus's trilogy. Taking the place of the antique chorus, young people of the present day question the traditional conception of the theatre.

11. SOPHOCLES: Antigonè (Antigone).

A rostrum surrounds the stage. The ground is covered with sand. The latter is at the same time the tomb of Polyneices, the passing of time, the dust of the ruins and the ashes employed in ritual ceremonies.

Helio EICHBAUER

14 - 17. SOPHOCLES: Antigonè (Antigone).

A general principle governs the relations between actors and spectators. The stage represents Thebes; the spectators are all Argives, with whom the Thebans are at war. The actors adopt an attitude of hostility towards the public, but seem at the same time to be consumed with fear. The actors playing the Elders or the people form a moving mass ready to change into a bird of prey, a wave of the sea, a machine of war, a Fascist monster. Here, the "Living Theatre" rejects lighting, setting and costumes; the actor must render everything by means of his body.

(Les Voies de la Création Théârale, Volume 1, Paris, CNRS, 1970)

35 - 39. EURIPIDES - THE PERFORMANCE GROUP: Bacchai Dionysus in 69.

The play text of *Dionysus in 69* is based on group improvisation: "We exchanged touches, places, ideas, anxieties, words, gestures, hostilities, rages, smells, glances, sounds, loves..."

Of the more than 1300 lines in Arrowsmith's translation of *The Bacchae,* we use nearly 600, some more than once. We also use sixteen lines from *Antigone* and six lines from *Hippolytus.* The rest of our text we made ourselves—some of it written at home, some worked out in workshop... Dionysus, from the very start of the play, says his own text, but as the play goes on, he moves closer and closer to Euripides' text. The opening ceremonies are of indeterminate duration. Their several functions overlap. The audience must be brought into an unusual theatre and initiated into an unusual space. A large space populated with towers and platforms. No clearly defined stage. The spectators can sit just about anywhere...

The core of the opening ceremonies is the first chorus, sung and said by the women, supported by the men. The men have only one line, addressed to the incoming audience, "Good evening, sir (ma'am), may I take you to your seat?". They also sound a base line—wails, cries, moans, rhythms. The chorus

is the sonic environment, and it is from this that the play precipitates as rain does from gathering clouds.

Richard SCHECHNER

The play is a series of revealments in which I find out that I am the God. By the time of the curse I am totally transformed.

The first transformation, going through the birth canal, is very important. It is a rite of passage toward Godhead.

Joan MacINTOSH (who played Dionysus)
(Dionysus in 69, The Performance Group, New York, The Noonday Press, 1970)

43 - 45. LUDOVICO ARIOSTO - EDOARDO SANGUINETI: Orlando Furioso.

Here, there is absolutely no distinction between the spectator's area and the actor's: the two areas intermingle, overlap, and penetrate each other. The different stage actions can develop at any point whatever of the rectangle, and often, as has been stated, at several points at once. The actors enter, as a rule, on trucks pushed from beneath, from behind or from the side by other players not being used for the time being, and they have to force their way through the spectators. These trucks are bare and carry either actors on their own or polished tin horses constructed somewhat after the manner of Sicilian puppets, a resemblance that is certainly not accidental. The fact is that these are stage machines that look what they are...

Ettore CAPRIOLO
(Théâtre des Nations, Paris, 1970)

50. WILLIAM SHAKESPEARE - JOHN BARTON: Wars of the Roses.

In this hard and dangerous world of our production, the central image—the steel of war—has spread and forged anew the whole of our medieval landscape. On the flagged floors of sheet steel, tables are daggers, staircases are axe-heads, and doors the traps on scaffolds. Nothing yields; stone walls have lost their seduction and now loom dangerously—steel-clad—to enclose and to imprison. The countryside offers no escape—the danger is still there in the iron foliage of the cruel trees and, surrounding all, the great steel cage of war.

John BURY

54 - 57. WILLIAM SHAKESPEARE: Romeo and Juliet.

The setting is provided by three trucks (loading capacity: 8 tons) and a supplementary wagon (2.7 square metres) for touring theatre. Each truck comprises a cubicle serving as dressing-room and a floor, behind the driver's seat, constituting the stage. The floor is 2.7 m. wide and 8.6 m. long. Three platforms are piled up on it: the upper can incline and slide, the lower can revolve 360 degrees. Lighting and sound equipment are located in the roof of the driver's cabin.

The Kanamori Corporation

61 - 67. WILLIAM SHAKESPEARE: A Midsummer Night's Dream.

The trapezes constitute what is no doubt the most striking feature of Brook's *Dream.* We wanted to delimit a specific small-sized acting area, a neutral place to introduce other elements of the play.

"There are points, for instance, where people are 'sleeping' while action is taking place. At first, we wanted the actors stuck on the walls, but didn't know how to do it. Then I suddenly realised that we already had a marvellous mechanism—the flies—for lifting the people up and down, and so the trapezes came in. They also accentuated the floating and dreaming aspect of the play. We could use the stage vertically as well as horizontally."

Sally JACOBS

74. WILLIAM SHAKESPEARE: As you like it.

An all male cast. Constant recourse to plastics and plexiglass for both setting and costumes: the style of the latter can be described as "modern timeless".

Ralph KOLTAI

75 - 78. WILLIAM SHAKESPEARE: As you like it.

The setting was conceived as a basic white plastic cube, that could be lit from within, giving reflections, or from behind, like a screen. Within this appeared 3 trees, mobile and self propelling. There was no ground plan, and the positions and movements of these "plastic forms" evolved during rehearsals.

Pamela HOWARD

123 - 125. WILLIAM SHAKESPEARE: Macbeth.

The Shakespeare lay-out conceived for *Macbeth* and *Julius Caesar* can also be utilized for other plays.

The principle is that of a functional setting which offers, right from the start, all the possibilities of transformation necessitated by the various moments of the various productions. As it constitutes a scenic apparatus rather than a setting, it has been made of highly finished materials (polished sycamore and unoxidizable brass), which recall those used for the construction of the apparatus formerly employed for teaching physics and astronomy.

The lay-out comprises five frames made of wooden beams joined together with struts; after assembly, it can be raised by hoisting all the elements simultaneously. Also pertaining to the lay-out, ten pivoting lateral sections which can be turned into circulatory side-galleries by lowering segments of the ceiling on to them. In *Macbeth,* the central segment of the ceiling (4 x 4 m.) became the banqueting table. The ceiling as a whole can be lowered to various levels: with the beams or the retractable floors of the podium-practicable, it then forms additional spaces. The podium can be made to tilt in keeping with the requirements of the production.

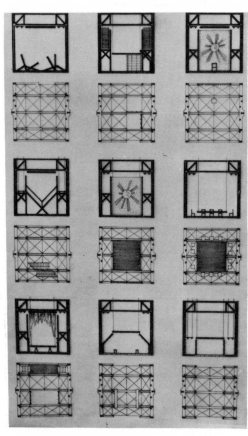

The inspiration for this lay-out can be found in the war-machines imagined by Leonardo da Vinci, but this is more a general impression than an attempted imitation.

Liviu CIULEI

162. MOLIERE: Le Malade imaginaire (The Imaginary Invalid).

The surface of the setting is covered, blanket-like, with a layer of wadding: this to give particular echo to the voices of the characters and to the sound of their footsteps. A thick felt carpet covers the stage-floor.

Laszlo SZEKELY

163 - 165. JEAN RACINE: Bérénice.

The setting evokes a drawing-room in a palace of an ideal society. This society is neither that of Rome, nor of the Versailles of Louis XIV. It represents the past. An idealized Louis XIII court with elements borrowed from Rome (the suits of armour), from Versailles (the mirrors), etc. In our opinion, this mirror-lined box presents a poetic correspondence with the way in which the characters address and question each other. They are there, reflected in their monologues and inscribed in the mirrors. Reality, cast back as in the mirrors, inversed. The mirrors multiply this uncertain world.

Roger PLANCHON
(*Cité Panorama n° 20*, Villeurbanne, 1970)

186. FRIEDRICH SCHILLER: Die Räuber (The Robbers).

Zadek and Minks show us *The Robbers* on an empty stage, before a circular horizon, on which the designer has painted a giant pastiche of a picture by American pop-artist Roy Lichtenstein. Lichtenstein extracts the elements of advertising and other strips from their context, enlarges them, lays them bare as it were, and aesthetizes them at the same time. It is a picture of this type that the designer has utilized.
The red and yellow hues, which seem to come straight from the two-colour pages of a cheap weekly, complete the transformation of the motif into a vulgar token of violence and sexuality.

Ernst WENDT

192. HENRIK IBSEN: Peer Gynt.

The setting represents the theatre in which Peer Gynt acts out the story of his life. The iron structure is entirely covered over with unhewn logs. The interstices between the logs provide a

means of lighting the different galleries, and enable the audience to see the life of the theatre behind the scene.

David SHARIR

212 - 213. ANTON CHEKHOV: Ivanov.

Everything must be seen through the eyes of Ivanov; what the public must be made to feel, by means of the scene shifts, is his frame of mind... The stage is almost bare. The change of atmosphere is indicated by projections, from various points of the stage, on the grey cyclorama, the grey curtains and the felt carpet.

Arpad CSANYI

223 - 224. STANISLAW WYSPIANSKY - JERZY GROTOWSKI: Akropolis (Acropolis).

The sacks which constitute the actors' garments, the apertures in them cut out with a flame-projector and the patches on them made of pieces of red and grey plastic material, the clogs and the dazzling spotlights, piercing the darkness of the house, also inundating the spectators seated near the players' zone of action, complete the production from the aesthetic angle.

242 - 244. OSWALDO DE ANDRADE: O Rei da Vela (The King of the Candle).

The rise and fall of a Brazilian money-lender around 1930. The dramatic action takes place within the framework of a critical realism involving major music-hall productions, opera and "technicolor" melodrama. Visible structures reveal the theatrical machine.

Helio EICHBAUER

246. LUCIAN BLAGA: Mesterul Manole (Master Builder Manole).

The utilization of unplaned, even unbarked wood, and of coarse holland, rough cloth and sheepskins for the costumes, constitutes an attempt to render the harsh and frugal atmosphere demanded by the text.
The setting, practicable at every level, is mounted exclusively by suspension, that is not fixed to the ground at any point. At the culminating moment of the performance, the entire structure is gradually hoisted up and disappears from sight, the lighting effects helping meanwhile to suggest a flight to the skies.

Sanda MUSATESCU

256. WILHELM MOBERG: Domaren (The Judge).

Scene-shifts during the performance took place noiselessly behind the panels, on which various pictures were projected. At the beginning of each scene, the projections came first, then the acting started. After each scene, one panel rose and another came down, concealing the setting which had just been utilized. And so on alternately.

Rolf STEGARS

278. BERTOLT BRECHT: Der gute Mensch von Sezuan (The Good Woman of Setzuan).

The "masks" are made of deforming elements covered with stockings.

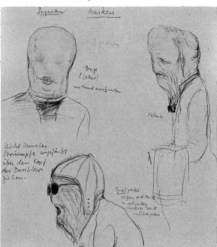

295. SAMUEL BECKET: En attendant Godot (Waiting for Godot).

The designer's problem was to provide a vast, open and undefined landscape, which would be at the same a place from which the characters could not easily get out or away. The solution was a continuous rake that ultimately defeats all attempts to run up it or off of it.
The rake is built of plywood covered over with sheets of tin-roofing recuperated in a scrap-yard. The colour of the set is that of naturally rusted tin. As the theatre is outdoors and open to the weather, the rust patina developed beautifully.

Stephen HENDRICKSON

302. JEAN ANOUILH: Antigone.

Creon's Palace of four shattered columns, being restored within a skeleton of modern steel scaffolding, is embedded on a ramped thrust stage projecting steeply into the audience. The scene suggests the ruins of war and the cage-like captivity of those living in a police state. During the play, the scaffolding becomes Antigone's prison.

Donald OENSLAGER

308. JEAN GENET: Le Balcon (The Balcony).

The basic setting with 3 rear projections screens as used throughout the performance : a total of 48 images were continuously projected by means of 6 projectors. For the last scene, the centre screen was raised and a large image overlapping 2 smaller screens was projected on the theatre's cyclorama.

J.S. OSTOJA - KOTKOWSKI

322. HANS HELLMUT KIRST - ERWIN PISCATOR: Aufstand der Offiziere (The Officers' Revolt).

Outcome of the experiment made by Piscator, forty years earlier, with *Rasputin*. This time, each segment of the sphere opens and closes rapidly, silently, operated by just one man. The closed sphere (16 m. in diametre, 8 m. high) becomes a film screen. Inside the cupola, a second surface for projections is constituted by the steel netting.
In Piscator's mind, this apparatus was to serve for a number of productions by reason of its exceptional adaptability.

Hans-Ulrich SCHMÜCKLE

326. ARTHUR MILLER: After the Fall.

Version for touring theatre. Scenic platforms, masking borders, wings and backdrop, as well as properties and dimming equipment, were carried in two trucks. In other words, all that was needed on the tour when arriving in a new town was an empty stage, a conventional rigging (flying) system and connections for lighting power to hook-up our totally portable system.

Jo MIELZINER

327-331. TADEUSZ HOLUJ: Puste Pole (Deserted Field).

The stage was used as an abstract space. It might have been an abandoned swimming-pool or an airfield. In this framework were grouped apparently disparate but judiciously chosen elements : metal wheelbarrows (raised here to the rank of partners), old dressmaker's dummies and artificial limbs, stove-pipes with projectors concealed inside them, motorcar wheels, etc. All these objects, just slightly touched up with paint, link up with the human being, form—together with man—a single and identical entity. The human being-actor dressed in a ragged sack constitutes the creative element of the production in both time and space.

Jozef SZAJNA

335-336. PETER WEISS: Marat-Sade.

This is my third version of *Marat-Sade*. All the spectators were seated more or less in the middle of the performance. The walls of the house were covered with the same tiles or design as the walls of the stage. White was the basic colour : some fifty shades of white in the costumes and the setting. The few touches of colour utilized stood out in contrast.

Gunilla PALMSTIERNA-WEISS

350. BENJAMIN GALAI : Sippur Uriah (The Story of Uriah).

A compact setting especially suited to small stages and high mobility touring. All the components and items of the set were fitted into a single background wall from which they were extracted during the successive scenes by the actors themselves. These actions of the actors were part of the play. The wall and the various elements were made of wood, the entire wall serving as a colourful background decorated with geometrical forms in orange, red and mauve.

Gila SCHAKHINE

354-358. OLE SARVIG : Kaspariana.
366-367. PETER SEEBERG : Ferai.

The auditorium (15 × 10 × 4 m.) is bare, without anything that even suggests a stage. For each of the Odin Teatret's productions, the auditorium is arranged in keeping with a new and well-defined plan ; the latter is aimed at establishing a fresh spatial relationship between the actors and the spectators and at activating the osmosis of the two groups concerned.
The entire auditorium is utilized as acting area and the director of the Odin Teatret tends to make use of the spectators as supernumeraries or as scenographic elements in building up the performance.
Number of spectators : a maximum of 90.

368-369. JAMES SAUNDERS : Dog Accident.

The setting was the most expensive ever—Marble Arch in London. A traffic island with benches around a small square directly in front of the Arch forms a perfect playing area. Access to this "island" is by subway, which means people are usually there intentionally. The spot was the original Tyburn site, where other outdoor dramas (state hangings) used to take place.
Dog Accident concerns two men en route to lunch who happen upon a dog hit by a car. One man wants to stay to see if he can help ; the other is in a hurry. Their ten minute scripted argument could be interfered with by the innocent bystanders (audience) and completely changed depending on what happened.
A stuffed, very realistic-looking dog, wired up to radio controls, which made it twitch, made this "play" real to those unsuspecting people who came to see what the commotion was about in front of Marble Arch.
I wanted the setting to have a majesty about it which would clearly point up a major issue of the play—the suffering of one small creature against the backdrop of man's immense accomplishments and tragedies.
This setting did not make the play into street theatre in any commonly accepted sense. Rather it was the selection of a "ready-made" perfect stage and using it as the environmental setting, totally integrating theme, audience, location, and players including one pitifully near-dead and macabre dog.

Ed BERMAN

376. EDWARD ALBEE: Tiny Alice.

The setting consists of two side-walls partially covered with slightly deforming mirrors. In the far background, a black and white image: this represents the site and is reflected in part of the walls in a peculiar manner. When the sacrificed Julian is shut up in the castle, and a few moments before the end, the side-walls come together in the distance: real space contracts while imaginary space expands.

Abd El Kader FARRAH

382. HAROLD PINTER : Silence.

A poem—glimpses of three people—three country people. Moments in time—moments in three lives. The constantly changing, but always recurring, imagery of sky, and wind, and countryside and darkness—and of faces reflected in the darkness. All scenic solutions constantly abandoned until the midnight lighting rehearsal and then a small miracle of the theatre. Three people suspended between mirror and sky, or sky and mirror, or mirror and mirror. No-one ever knew which.

John BURY

383. JOSE TRIANA : La Noche de los Asesinos (The Assassins).

Expressionist setting in the shape of an attic, where children are playing the game of murderers and their trial, watched over by ghosts. Furniture of inordinate size, sprung from the memories of childhood.

Helio EICHBAUER

387 - 389. ISTVAN EÖRSI : A hordok (The Barrels).

The action, situated during and after World War II, takes place "above" and "below" : "above" being in an apartment, in the street, etc., "below" being in a shelter or in the barrel which constitutes the hero's hiding-place. This barrel is the keystone of the drama : the plane of the world "above" is consequently balancing on the barrel "below". This balancing plane can be stabilized but at a given signal it frees itself and follows the movement of the actors who are on it.
All the rostrums are covered with black velvet and placed against a black background ; the balancing plane is also black. The furniture, all white, is lowered on to the stage from the flies.

Gabor SZINTE

394 - 396. FERNANDO ARRABAL : Le Cimetière des Voitures (The Automobile Graveyard).

Garcia wished to stage "a mechanized scrap-yard of the year 2000, distorted, derisory like the Chaplinesque satires of the days of the silent film". It is the derisory image of the world of each one of us, it is "the church, the hearth, the place where one loves, where one rends the beloved, the torture chamber, the place where one lives, if you get me". For Garcia, there was no question of staging the production in what is commonly called a theatre. The carcasses of the cars did not lend themselves to a proscenium-arch stage. According to the plans, 18 m. × 12.5 m. in height were required, and the spectators had to be integrated into the action.

(Les Voies de la Création Théâtrale, Vol. 1, Paris, C.N.R.S., 1970)

414. FREDERIC BAAL : Real Reel.

No story. "Scenic moments" following each other without any logical link to connect them up. So one passes suddenly from one situation to another, advancing—without progressing—from one unknown to the next.
The accessories : a reeling machine—two lengths of iron piping—an iron ring—two metal knees—a billiard ball.

Frédéric BAAL

415. HENRI KAPULAINEN : Nainen Ystävä (Her Friend).

Birth : The birth of a child was made objective by comparing the event and the ritual way of acting with the production and marketing of industrial articles.
Mother's Day : One day per year, this exploited member of the family is the centre of honour and traditional rituals. All this is rendered macabre by the mode of acting.
Any space on floor or platform measuring 3 × 2.5 m. will do for the performance.
Setting : 4 "seating" elements of about 50 × 50 × 50 cm. each : 1 element used, according to requirements, as kitchen closet, tombstone, catafalque, writing-table, bed, etc., and as the box containing the accessories.
The main objective was to produce a relatively cheap, lightweight and easily transportable (to factories, schools, meetings) theatrical introduction to discussion with the public.

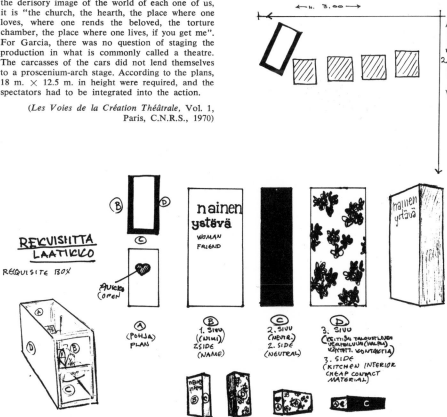

401 - 402. LeROI JONES : Slave Ship.

I had to rip up the seats, and level the floor of the Chelsea Theatre Centre. In the center a large platform was constructed on rockers. The audience peers into the narrow space below, to observe the tortured slave cargo ; frightened, screaming, vomiting, crying, giving birth. Jone's "Ship" is a metaphor, a symbol, connecting the memory of African roots with the vicious containment of the present. The ship is the fulcrum from which the play moves backward and forward in time. Gill Moses staged the piece in a very free theatrical style, action occurring throughout the room. Smells ... incense ... squeaking ... sea smells, urine / dirt / filth smells / bodies ... EXCREMENT, DEATH ... LIFE, groovy ...

Eugene LEE

419 - 420. THE LIVING THEATRE : Frankenstein.

The framework provided for *Frankenstein* consists of a structure in metal tubing 6 m. high and 10 m. wide ; it is divided into 15 compartments and stands at the back of the stage.
The dead leave their places and come together to form the "Creature" : one actor, crouched down and training two red lights on the public, for the head ; three standing and two squatting players for the trunk ; four for the legs and arms. Those representing the arms are attached by the waist to a hook located under the third level ; their legs lie on the shoulders of the actors forming the trunk, their heads are pendent. The position of those forming the legs is such that the latter are slightly apart. The "Creature" moves.

(Les Voies de la Création Théâtrale, Vol. 1, Paris, C.N.R.S., 1970)

421 - 423. THE OTHER COMPANY : The Pit.

The design of *The Pit* was intended to be the concrete and fairly integrated realization of the aims and areas of exploration set before TOC. These are :
1) The ideal of group work.
2) The concept of environmental theatre.
3) The performer-audience relationship.
4) The re-examination of the social function of the theatre.

The Pit is a rectangular box made of wood and canvas measuring 20' × 12' × 6'.
The physical unfolding of this structure is experienced physically as well as mentally by the audience.

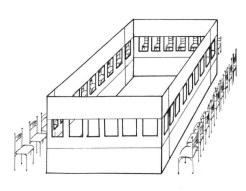

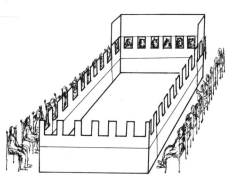

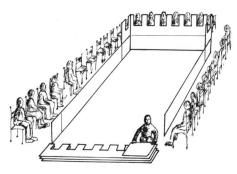

Spectators and actors are free to choose between two courses : that of re-erecting the pit around themselves (which happened on several occasions), that of using the whole open and free space to explore new possibilities.

Naftali YAVIN

424. BREAD AND PUPPET THEATRE : Fire.

The following scene (*Thursday*) is one of uncanny power. The figures are seated, facing each other, in a double row going from the front of the stage to the back. A new-comer apppears among them, bound with a heavy rope. The sensitive, groping hands reach out to him. The attention of the sightless eyes reflects a sort of wonder. His hands, too, fall awkwardly against the rope ... until, after failing and failing again, all these hands have finally freed him. He stands in the center of the stage and holds out the rope for all to see. We do see it. The rope is uncanny. The bell tolls and the curtain is drawn across.
The *Friday* stage is in darkness. A figure turns on an overhead light. The one who was freed of the rope lies under covers on a cot. Another sits on a chair beside him. Others hover in the background. A loud rattling is heard off-stage. The

seated figure rises and the others come forward. They look long at the one on the cot ... then lift the covers and drawn them slowly over his face. The bell tolls.

George DENNISON
(*The Drama Review*, 47,
New York University, 1970)

425. BREAD AND PUPPET THEATRE : The Cry of the People for Meat.
Cain's Birth.

The expulsion scene changes, somehow, into another in which Adam seems to be delivering Eve from an attacker with a beast's head, pulling him off her and out of his beast-mask, he clinging to her or she to him. With slow and sweeping gestures, the Angel proceeds to strike the attacker elaborately. The latter is on the ground, his arms and legs sticking up (an ancient gag from burlesque and puppet theatre, but frightful here) ; the Angel keeps striking them down, he will not die ... he is flat on the ground, slain. But he comes to life again, immediately ! He rises !
The whole scene, although manifestly a reference to Cain, is very confused : a mixture of rape, birth, homicide, rescue—images of Divine Wrath, procreation, strife, and survival. According to Schumann, Eve gives birth, a beast crawls up, she grabs its head, the man Adam pulls Cain out. He is born, but he is not yet alive. The Angel strikes him alive, He is Cain.

Stefan BRECHT
(*The Drama Review*, 47,
New York University, 1970)

459. ARNOLD SCHÖNBERG : Moses und Aron (Moses and Aaron).

The action takes place in the void where the spirit of God beams forth. The setting is thus reduced to a single, effulgent point. The latter determines the median axis. A blinding light emanates from this point when Moses realizes intuitively that he is called on to prophesy by the spirit of God. The light fades and grows dim when the spirit of God is misunderstood or misinterpreted.

Heinrich WENDEL

460. ARNOLD SCHÖNBERG : Die Jacobsleiter (Jacob's Ladder).

It was necessary to provide the illusion of a vast space through which the "souls" could float, appear, disappear and finally enter Heaven. The problem was solved by the use of abstract silvery "clouds" made of lucite and silver leaf, which could be lighted through and projected upon to change the shape and size of the stage space through light.

Neil Peter JAMPOLIS

465. IGOR STRAVINSKIJ : Oedipus Rex.

Seven ramps intersect at the centre of the stage : a ramp for each of the five principal characters and two for Oedipus—one for his entrance and one, crossing the centre, for his exit. The chorus is static, in an elliptical formation, at the base of the monolithic, 16-metre high walls. In plan, the set forms an ellipse.
The exaggerated texture, in high relief, is made of mulched wood splinters and chunks of styro-foam embedded in expandable polyurethane foam on wire-mesh frames. The monumental ritual masks are sculpted in polyurethane foam.

John EZELL

484. CARL ORFF : Prometheus.

Svoboda's scenography for Carl Orff's *Prometheus* can be regarded as the synthesis of some of his major orientations : monumental constructions, scenic kinetics, the dramatic of light, recourse to televised images.
From minus 2.16 m., a staircase, facing the public and extending rearward over the entire width of the stage, rises to a height of plus 8.8 m. ; at the height of plus 4 m., it divides into two dissymmetrical sections with a wedge-shaped opening between them ; a mobile, rhomboidal parallelepiped of enormous size can be made to slide through this opening. Of abstract form and irregular geometrical conception, this rhomboid— which pursues a horizontal course corresponding to the stage-house axis—is, in fact, the legendary rock with Prometheus chained to its forefront. Thanks to its mobility, the parallelepiped can

move 7 m. forward above the orchestra-pit, and thus place the isolated hero under the eyes of the public.

Denis BABLET
(*Svoboda*, Lausanne, La Cité, 1970)

485. KURT WEILL : Aufstieg und Fall der Stadt Mahagonny (The Rise and Fall of the City Mahagonny).

This production did not set out to present the work as a period piece, but to stress its relevance to the present time. The costumes were modern (1963), and a threefold projection screen at the rear of the stage was employed to make contemporary political comments relating to the action.

Ralph KOLTAI

498. MORDECHAI SETTER : Nashim Ba'Ohel (Women in the Tent).

a) An iron structure, movable and revolving during the dance, symbolizes Abraham's tamarisk tree.
b) A tent-like form, built in the course of the dance, assumes different aspects through the changes brought to a piece of cloth.

Dani KARAVAN

505 - 507. BERND ALOIS ZIMMERMANN : Die Soldaten (The Soldiers).

For *The Soldiers*, the acting area comprises five sections which can be utilized conjointly, separately, or by groups. These sections are : the front of the stage which constitutes a sort of apron ; two raised scenic "boxes", in close proximity but not directly interconnected, which are used either open, or closed by means of screens ; the two platforms constituted by the tops of these "boxes".

Denis BABLET
(*Svoboda*, Lausanne, La Cité, 1970)

513 - 515. LUIGI NONO : Intolleranza (Intolerance).

Given the ultimate horrors of the intolerant world Nono depicts, where the scale of human suffering is beyond size, Svoboda has used a simple concept of black-and-white projections on as many as five vast screens, which slide silently down from the flys and hover about the empty, raked stage.
A pictorial record of intolerance is flashed upon the screens, with documentary stills sometimes spaced with filmed-tape of simultaneous stage action. The stills (bodies and bones piled up in a concentration camp ; a man bloodied and frozen in death on a wall ; a Negro whipped while chained to a tree ; a grim, restive strike mob) are most often projected in the negative, occasionally in positive, and the effect is like a nightmare shifting from ugly reality to a kind of brute fantasy.

Kevin KELLY
(*The Boston Globe*, 22-2-1965)

528 - 532. GIACOMO MANZONI : Atomtod (Atomic Death).

The scenography for *Atomic Death* was based on a 8 × 8 × 3 m. structure destined to move downstage and composed of hollow aluminium spheres. The latter were riddled with 5 mm. holes and thus became 60 % transparent when lit from behind. The structure looked like concrete when lit from the front but gave an impression of weightlessness and transparency when lit from behind.
As the spheres were coated with grey paint containing some 30 % of bronze, they lent themselves to the projection of films and diapositives. Movement was imparted to the still projections by the downstage progress of the structure. In addition to the latter, a system of variable screens set admidst the black velvet of the proscenium arch allowed for the projection of multiple-screen films. Furthermore, there slid in from the wings a spheroid measuring 3 m. in diameter which comprised eight duralumin facets and a circular platform with a diameter of 2.50 m. These facets revolved on their axis seventy times per minute and thus formed a semi-transparent, spherical screen. Beside these three basic elements, other structures appeared from the wings in various counter-movements and constituted, together with the projection of films and diapositives, the scenography of the opera.

Joseph SVOBODA
(*World Theatre*, XV - 1, Paris, Brient, 1966)

SELECTIVE BIBLIOGRAPHY OF THE WORKS PUBLISHED SINCE 1960

Some time ago, we requested the National I.T.I. Centres to supply a list of the works devoted to stage design (and accessorily to the place of production, the costume, etc...) published in their country since 1960.

Although the resulting documentation presents serious gaps—the countries of Asia, the Spanish-speaking nations...—we were unwilling to deprive our readers of this abundant, varied and original information of which the equivalent cannot be easily found.

We have adopted a simple classification which permits the grouping of works of the most diverse origins.

*

In each country, highly qualified experts kindly agreed to establish the initial selections :

Ned A. Bowman and Carol Solomon (Arts Information International, Pittsburgh) for the United States, David Cheshire for the United Kingdom, Friedrich Dieckmann (OISTT) for the German Democratic Republic, Gerda Dietrich for the Federal Republic of Germany, Aleksandra Kurczab for Italy, Elena Rakitina for the U.S.S.R.

The selections established by these experts comprised not only complete works but also articles from periodicals : lack of space has obliged us to omit the latter.

We extend our thanks to all those who have completed or corrected our data : Armand Delcampe and Carlos Tindemans for Belgium, Suzanne Gal for Hungary, Cécile Giteau for France, Zygmunt Hübner for Poland, Ingrid Luterkort for Sweden, Tuomo Tirkkonen for Finland.

I. STAGE DESIGN

(Its materialization, its aesthetics, its history. The designers)

AKHRAMOVITCH-BOGOMOLOVA, M. : *Stsenitcheskie materialy v teatralno-dekoratsionnom iskousstve.* Moskva, VTO, 1965. ALEXANDRE, Arsene : *The decorative art of Leon Bakst. Appreciation by Arsene Alexandre. Notes on the ballets by Jean Cocteau. Translated from the French by Harry Melvill.* New York, B. Blom, 1971 (Reprint). ALPATOV, M. : *E. Gounst, N.N. Sapounov.* Moskva, Iskousstvo, 1965. ANATOMIE... *Anatomie d'une illusion. Essais du décor de théâtre au XIXe siècle. Anatomy of an illusion. Studies in nineteenth-century scene design.* Amsterdam, Scheltema & Holkema, 1969. (Conférences du quatrième Congrès International de Recherches Théâtrales, Amsterdam 1965). ARKKITEHTILEHTI... *Arkkitehtilehti 10-11/67 (magazin).* [Helsinki], 1967.

BABLET, Denis : *Esthétique générale du décor de théâtre de 1870 à 1914.* Paris, Centre National de la Recherche Scientifique, 1965. BABLET, Denis : *Josef Svoboda.* Lausanne, La Cité, 1970. BARTOLUCCI, Giùseppe : *La scrittura scenica.* Roma, Lerici, 1968. BASSEKHES, A. : *Khoudojniki na stsene MKHAT.* Moskva, VTO, 1960. BASSEKHES, A. : *Teatralno-dekoratsionnoe iskousstvo 1934-1941 godov. — « Istoriia rousskogo iskousstva »,* t. 12. Moskva, AN SSSR, 1961. BASSEKHES, A. : *A. Ia. Golovin.* Moskva, Sovietskij khoudojnik, 1970. BAZANOV, V. : *Stsena, tekhnika, spektakl.* Leningrad, Iskousstvo, 1963. BAZANOV, V. : *Teatralnaia tekhnika v obraznom reshenii spektaklia.* Moskva, Iskousstvo, 1970. BENOIS, Alexandre : *Memoirs. Translated by Moura Budberg.* 2 vol. London, Chatto & Windus, 1960-1964. BENOUA, Alexandr (Alexandre Benois) : *Alexandr Benoua razmyshlaet. Sbornik statej. 1917-1960.* Moskva, Sovietskij khoudojnik, 1968. BEREZKIN, V. : *Khoudojnik i spektakl.* Moskva, Znanie, 1967. BEREZKIN, V. : *Khoudojnik v sovremennom teatre.* Moskva, Znanie, 1970. BERGMAN, Gösta M. : *Den moderna teaterns genombrott 1890-1925.* Stockholm, Bonnier, 1966. BESKIN, O. : *Iourij Pimenov.* Moskva, Sovietskij khoudojnik, 1960. BESKIN, O. : *V. Shestakov.* Moskva, Sovietskij khoudojnik, 1965. BJURSTRÖM, Per : *Giacomo Torelli and baroque stage design.* Stockholm, Almqvist & Wiksell, 1961. BJURSTRÖM, Per : *Teaterdekoration i Sverige.* Stockholm, Natur & Kultur, 1964. BOSSAGLIA, Rossana : *I fratelli Galliari pittori.* Milano, Ceschina, 1962. BÜHNENBILDARBEIT... *Bühnenbildarbeit in der Deutschen Demokratischen Republik. Mit Texten von Karl von Appen, Heinrich Kilger, Andreas Reinhardt, Reinhart Zimmermann sowie 61 Abb. von dem DDR-Beitrag zur Prager Quadriennale. Herausgegeben von Friedrich Dieckmann.* Berlin, Sektion DDR der OISTT, 1971. BURIAN, Jarka : *Scenography of Josef Svoboda.* Middletown (Conn.), Wesleyan Univ. Press, 1971. BURRIS-MEYER, Harold and COLE, Edward : *Scenery for the theatre. Second edition.* Boston, Little, Brown and Co., 1971.

[CHANEL, P.] : *Christian Bérard décorateur. Catalogue d'exposition (Nancy, 22 avril - 30 mai 1966).* CHENEY, Sheldon : *Stage decoration.* New York, B. Blom, 1966 (Reprint). CLARK, Frank D. : *Special effects in motion pictures.* New York, Society of Motion Picture and Television Engineers, 1966. COOPER, Douglas : *Picasso theatre.* New York, H. N. Abrams, 1968. COREY, Irene : *The mask of reality ; an approach to design for theatre.* Anchorage (Ky), Anchorage Press, 1968. COURTNEY, Richard : *Stage craft.* Huddersfield, Union, 1960.

DAVYDOVA, M. : *Teatralno-dekoratsionnoe iskousstvo kontsa XIX - natchala XX veka. « Istoriia rousskogo iskousstva »,* tom 10, kn. 2. Moskva, Naouka, 1969. DAVYDOVA, M. : *Teatralno-dekoratsionnaia i dekorativnaia jivopis vtoroj poloviny XVIII veka. « Istoriia rousskogo iskousstva »,* t. 7. Moskva, AN SSSR, 1961. DAVYDOVA, M. : *Teatralno-dekoratsionnaia i dekorativnaia jivopis pervoj poloviny XIX veka. « Istoriia rousskogo iskousstva »,* t. 8, kn. 2. Moskva, Naouka, 1964. DECOR... *Le décor de théâtre dans le monde depuis 1950. Textes et illustrations rassemblés par les Centres Nationaux de l'I.I.T., choisis et présentés par René Hainaux, avec les conseils techniques d'Yves-Bonnat. Avant-propos par P.-L. Mignon.* Paris-Bruxelles, Meddens, 1964. DECOR... *Le décor de théâtre dans le monde depuis 1935. Textes et illustrations rassemblés par les Centres Nationaux de l'I.I.T., choisis et présentés par René Hainaux, avec les conseils techniques d'Yves-Bonnat. Préface par Kenneth Rae. Deuxième édition.* Bruxelles, Meddens, 1970 (Réimpression). DECORATEURS... *Décorateurs de théâtre tchécoslovaques 1960-1970. Designers of the Czechoslovak theatres 1960-1970.* Praha, Divadelni Ustav, 1971. DE'SOMMI, Leone : *Quattro dialoghi in materia de rappresentazioni sceniche.* Milano, Il Polifilo, 1968. DIECKMANN, Friedrich : *Karl von Appens Bühnenbilder am Berliner Ensemble.* Berlin, Henschelverlag, 1971. DOKOUTCHAEVA, V. : *I. Nivinskij.* Moskva, Sovietskij khoudojnik, 1969. DRAMATEN... *Dramaten 175 år. Studier i svensk scenkonst. Red. av. Gösta M. Bergman och Niklas Brunius.* Stockholm, Norstedt, 1963.

EATON, Quaintance : *Opera production, a handbook.* Minneapolis, University of Minnesota Press, 1961. EPSTEIN, John and others comp. : *The black box : an experiment in visual theatre.* London, Latimer, 1970. ERENGROSS, B. : *Khoudojnik v teatre.* Moskva, VTO, 1962. ERFAHRUNGEN... *Erfahrungen aus der Regiearbeit. Berichte, Aufsätze, Studien. — Kap. VI : Das Bild spielt mit. Studienmaterial der Spezialschule für Leiter des künstlerischen Volksschaffens, Fachgebiet Laientheater.* Leipzig, Zentralhaus für Kulturarbeit, 1969. ETKIND, M. : *A.N. Benoua (Benois).* Leningrad-Moskva, Iskousstvo, 1965. ETKIND, M. : *Akimov - khoudojnik.* Leningrad, Khoudojnik RSFSR, 1960. ETKIND, M. : *B. M. Koustodiev.* Leningrad-Moskva, Iskousstvo, 1960.

FUERST, Walter René and HUME, Samuel J. : *Twentieth-century stage decoration* [by] *Walter René Fuerst and Samuel J. Hume. With an introd. by A. Appia.* New York, B. Blom, 1967 (Reprint). FUNKE, Christoph, HOFFMANN-OSTWALD, Daniel und OTTO, Hans-Gerald : *Theaterbilanz 1945-1969. Eine Dokumentation über die Bühnen der Deutschen Demokratischen Republik.* Berlin, Henschelverlag, 1971.

GALLI BIBIENA, Giuseppe : *Architectural and perspective designs dedicated to His Majesty Charles VI, Holy Roman Emperor, by Giuseppe Galli da Bibiena. With an introd. by A. Hyatt Mayor.* New York, Dover pub., 1964 (Reprint). GILLETTE, Arnold S. : *Stage scenery.* New York, Harper & Row Pub., 1960. GILLETTE, Arnold S. : *An introduction to stage design* [by] *A.S. Gillette.* London, Harper & Row, 1967. GITEAU, Cécile: *Dictionnaire des Arts du Spectacle.* Paris, Dunod, 1970. GOLLANCZ, Victor : *Ring at Bayreuth.* New York, Dutton, E. P. & Co., 1966. GOLOVIN, A. : *Vstretchi i vpetchatleniia. Pisma. Vospominanniia o Golovine.* Leningrad-Moskva, Iskousstvo, 1960. GORBATCHEV, D. : *A. Petritskij.* Moskva, Sovietskij khoudojnik, 1970.

HEARTFIELD, John : *Leben und Werk. Dargestellt von seinem Bruder Wieland Herzfelde. Mit über 300 einfarb. u. mehrfarb. Abb. 2 Aufl.* Dresden, VEB Verlag der Kunst, 1971. HISTOIRE... *Histoire du lieu et du décor de théâtre. 90 diapositives. Commentaires d'Henriette Boulay et Lucienne Depraets.* Paris, Ligue de l'Enseignement, 1966. HÖGER, Gudrun, e.a. : *Bühnentechnik - Beleuchtung - Requisit. Sudienmaterial der Spezialschule für Leiter des künstlerischen Volksschaffens, Fachgebiet Laientheater.* Leipzig, Zentralhaus für Kulturarbeit, 1961 u. 1965. HURME, J., VASARA, E., STEGARS, R., HEISKANEN, P. : *Lavastus. (Finnish Stage Design).* Helsinki (SKK), Suomen Lavastustaiteilijain Liitto (Association of the Finnish Stage Designers), 1962.
JEUDWINE, Wynne : *Stage designs.* Fetham, Country Life Books, 1968. JONES, Robert Edmond : *Drawings for the theatre. Second edition.* New York, Theatre Arts Books, 1970. JOSEPH, Stephen : *Scene painting and design. With a foreword by Sean Kenny.* London, Pitman, 1964. JUNG, Otto : *Der Theatermaler Friedrich Christian Benther (1777-1856) und seine Welt.* Emsdetten, Verlag Lechte, 1963.

KAISER, Hermann : *Der Bühnenmeister Carl Brandt und Richard Wagner. Kunst und Szene in Darmstadt und Bayreuth.* Darmstadt, Verlag Roether, 1968. KAPRALOV, B. : *B. M. Koustodiev. Stati. Zametki. Interviou.* Leningrad, Khoudojnik RSFSR, 1967. KNIAZEVA, V. : *N. Rerikh.* Leningrad-Moskva, Iskousstvo, 1968. KOGAN, D. : *Golovin.* Moskva, Iskousstvo, 1960. KOMAROVSKAIA, N. I. : *Korovin.* Moskva, Iskousstvo, 1964. KOMMISSARZHEVSKII, Fedor Fedorovich and SIMONSON, Lee : *Settings and costumes of the modern stage.* New York, B. Blom, 1966 (Reprint). KOOK, Edward F. : *Images in light for the living theatre.* New York, Edward F. Kook, 1963. KOROVIN, Konstantin : *Jizn i tvortchestvo. Pisma. Dokoumenty. Vospominaniia. Moskva,* izdatelstvo Akademii khoudojestv, 1963. KOSTINA, E. : *Fiodor Fiodorovitch Federovskij.* Moskva, Sovietskij khoudojnik, 1960. KOUMANKOV, E. : *V. E. Egorov.* Moskva, Soviejtskij khoudojnik, 1965.

La NIER-KUHNT, Irmhilt : *Philosophie und Bühnenbild. Leben und Werk des Szenikers Hans Wildermann.* Emsdetten, Verlag Lechte, 1971. LARSON, Orville Kurth : *Scene design for stage and screen : readings on the aesthetics and methodology of scene design for drama, opera, musical comedy, ballet, motion pictures, television and arena theatre.* East Lansing, Michigan State University Press, 1961. LEBEDEVA, V. : *B. M. Koustodiev.* Moskva, Naouka, 1966. LENTOULOVA, M. : *Khoudojnik Aristarkh Lentoulov.* Moskva, Sovietskij khoudojnik, 1970. LIPOVITCH, I. : *I. Ia. Bilibin.* Leningrad, Khoudojnik RSFSR, 1966. LOUTSKAIA, E. : *Teatralno-dekoratsionnoe iskousstvo. «Istoriia rousskogo iskousstva»,* tom XIII. Moskva, Naouka, 1964.

MANCINI, Franco : *Scenografia italiana dal Rinascimento all'eta romantica. Testo di Franco Mancini.* Milano, Fratelli Fabbri, 1966. MARCHI, Virgilio : *Note sulla scenografia. Vol. I : Propedeutica.* Roma, Centro sperimentale di Cinematografia, s.d. MEDVEDEV, B., SYRKINA, F. : *Teatralno-dekoratsionnoe iskousstvo 1917-1934 godov. «Istoriia rousskogo iskousstvo», tom 12.* Moskva, AN SSSR, 1961. MELVILL, Harald : *Designing and painting scenery for the theatre.* Chester Springs (Pa.), Dufour Editions, 1963. MIELZINER, Jo : *Designing for the theatre. A memoir and a portfolio.* New York, Atheneum, 1965. MIKHAJLOVA, A. : *Khoudojnik v mouzykalnom teatre. Sbornik «Mouzykalnyj teatr i sovremennost. Voprosy razvitiia sovietskoj opery».* Moskva, VTO, 1962. MIKHAJLOVA, A. : *I.V. Sevastianov.* Leningrad, Khoudojnik RSFSR, 1962. MILLER, James H. : *Self-supporting scenery.* Shreveport (Louisiana), E. T. Tobey Co., 1971. MOLINARI, Cesare : *Spettacoli fiorentini del Quattrocento.* Venezia, Neri Pozza, 1961. MOLINARI, Cesare : *Le nozze degli dei.* Roma, Bulzoni, 1968. MOUSSINAC, Leon : *The new movement in the theatre ; a survey of recent developments in Europe and America. With an introd. by R.H. Packman and a foreword by Gordon Craig.* New York, B. Blom, 1967 (Reprint).
NEKHOROSHEV, Iou : *Khoudojnik i stsena.* Moskva, Iskousstvo, 1964. NELMS, Henning : *Scene design ; a guide to the stage.* New York, Sterling Pub. Co., 1970. NOGUCHI, Isamu : *A sculptor's world.* London, Thames & Hudson, 1967.

OENSLAGER, Donald : *Scenery then and now.* New York, Russel & Russel, 1966 (Reprint). ONOUFRIEVA, S. : *A. Ia. Golovin. Teatralnye èskizy. Albom.* Leningrad, Khoudojnik RSFSR, 1961. ONOUFRIEVA, S. : *A. Ia. Golovin.* Leningrad, Khoudojnik RSFSR, 1966. ORIENTAMENTI... *Orientamenti della scenografia. A cura di «Prospettive». Seconda edizione.* Milano, Görlich, 1965. OTTO, Teo : *Meine Szene.* Köln-Berlin, Verlag Kiepenheuer und Witsch, 1965.

PARKER, W. Oren : *Sceno-graphic techniques.* Pittsburgh, Carnegie-Mellon, 1964. PARKER, Wilford Oren and SMITH, Harvey K. : *Scene design and stage lighting. Second edition.* New York, Holt, Rinehart & Winston, 1968. PHILIPPS, Peter, Lawrence : *An iconography of American scene design, 1920-1935.* Los Angeles, 1966. PIATDESIAT... *Piatdesiat let sovietskogo iskousstva. Khoudojniki teatra.* Moskva, Sovietskij khoudojnik, 1969. POJARSKAIA, M. : *N. N. Medovshtchikov.* Leningrad, Khoudojnik RSFSR, 1960. POJARSKAIA, M. : *Rousskoe teatralno-dekoratsionnoe iskousstvo kontsanatchala XX veka.* Moskva, Iskousstvo, 1970. POJARSKAIA, M. : *Nisson Shifrin.* Moskva, Sovietskij khoudojnik, 1971. POVOLEDO, Elena : *Una rapprezentazione academica a Venezia nel 1634.* Firenze, Olschki, 1971.

QUADRIENNALE... *Quadriennale de Prague de décors et d'architecture théâtraux. Prague quadrennial of theatre design and architecture, 1967.* Praha, Divadelni Ustav, s.d. QUADRIENNALE... *Quadriennale de Prague de décors et d'architecture théâtraux. Prague quadrennial of theatre design and architecture, 1971.* Praha, Divadelni Ustav, 1971.

RAKITINA, E. : *Anatolij Afanasievitch Arapov.* Moskva, Sovietskij khoudojnik, 1966. RAKITINA, E. : *I. Shlepianov - khoudojnik obnovlennogo teatra. «Voprosy teatra».* Moskva, VTO, 1967. RAKITINA, E. : *Novye printsipy stsenitcheskogo oformleniia v sovietskoj teatralnoj dekoratsii 1920-kh godov. Avtoreferat.* Moskva, Institout istorii iskousstv Ministerstva koultoury SSSR, 1970. REINKING, Wilhelm : *Verzeichnis meiner Arbeiten 1924-1964.* München, Laokoon, 1964. RICHTER, Horst : *Johann Oswald Harms. Ein deutscher Theaterdekorateur des Barock.* Emsdetten, Verlag Lechte, 1963. RIESER, Willy : *Toneeltekeningen.* 's-Gravenhage, Stols, 1961. RISCHBIETER, Henning und STORCH, Wolfgang : *Bühne und bildende Kunst im XX. Jahrhundert. Maler und Bildhauer arbeiten für das Theater.* Velber bei Hannover, Friedrich Verlag, 1968. ROWELL, Kenneth : *Stage design.* London, Studio Vista, 1968. RYNDIN, V. : *Kak sozdaetsia khoudojestvennoe oformlenie spektalia.* Moskva, izdatelstvo Akademii khoudojestv SSSR, 1962. RYNDIN, V. : *Khoudojnik i teatr.* Moskva, VTO, 1966.

SAGERT, Horst : *Bühnenbilder und Figurinen zu Jewgeni Schwarz' «Der Drache». Hrsg. u. nachwort von Lothar Lang. 21 farbige Bildtafeln.* Leipzig, Insel-Verlag Anton Kippenberg, 1971. SCENOGRAFIA... *Scenografia românesca. Stage design in Rumania. La scénographie roumaine.* Bucuresti, Meridiane, 1965. SCHOLZ, Janos : *Baroque and romantic stage design.* New York, E. P. Dutton, 1962. SELIVANOV, V. : *Teatralnaia mebel.* Moskva, Iskousstvo, 1960. SHERINGHAM, George and LAVER, James : *Design in the theatre.* New York, B. Blom, s.d. (Reprint). SHIFRIN, N. : *Khoudojnik v teatre.* Leningrad, Khoudojnik RSFSR, 1964. SHIFRIN, N. : *Moia rabota v teatre.* Moskva, Sovietskij khoudojnik, 1966. SHLEPIANOV, I. : *Sbornik statej.* Moskva, Iskousstvo, 1969. SIMONSON, Lee : *The stage is set.* New York, Theatre Arts Books, 1964 (Reprint). SOSSOUNOV, N. : *Ot maketa k dekoratsii.* Moskva, Iskousstvo, 1962. SOUTHERN, Richard : *Stage setting for amateurs and professionals. Second ed.* London, Faber, 1964. SPENCER, Charles : *Erte.* London, Studio Vista, 1970. STAGE... *Stage design throughout the world since 1935. Texts and illustrations collected by the National Centers of the International Theatre Institute chosen and presented by René Hainaux with the technical advice of Yves-Bonnat. Sketch to serve as foreword by Jean Cocteau. Preface by Kenneth Rae.* New York, Theatre Arts Books, 1965 (Reprint). STAGE... *Stage design throughout the world since 1950. Texts and illustrations collected by the National Centers of the International Theatre Institute chosen and presented by René Hainaux with the technical advice of Yves-Bonnat. Foreword by Paul-Louis Mignon.* New York, Theatre Arts Books, 1964. STEINBECK, Dietrich : *Richard Wagners «Tannhäuser» Szenarium. Das Vorbild der Erstaufführungen mit der Kostümbeschreibung und den Dekorationsskizzen.* West-Berlin, Selbstverlag der Gesellschaft für Theatergeschichte, 1968. STRAVINSKI... *Stravinski and the theatre, a catalogue of decor and costume designs for stage productions of his works, 1910-1962.* New York, New York Public Library, 1963. STRAZZULLO, Franco : *Contributi al periodo napoletano dello scenografo Domenico Chelli.* Napoli, 1962. STRZELECKI, Zenobiusz : *Kierunki scenografii wspolczesnej.* Warszawa, Panstwowy Instytut Wydawniczy, 1970. STRZELECKI, Zenobiusz : *Polska plastyka teatralna.* Warszawa, Panstwowy Instytut Wydawniczy, 1963. SYRKINA, F. : *Teatralno-dekoratsionnoe iskousstvo vtoroj poloviny XIX veka. «Istoriia rousskogo iskousstva», tom 9, kniga 2.* Moskva, Naouka, 1965. SYRKINA, F. : *A. Ia. Tyshler.* Moskva, Sovietskij khoudojnik, 1967. SZCENOGRAFIA... *Szcenografia I.* Budapest, Szinhaztudomanyi Intézet, 1960. SZCENOGRAFIA... *Szcenografia II.* Budapest, Szinhaztudomanyi Intézet, 1960. SZCENOGRAFIA... *Szcenografia III.* Budapest, Szinhaztudomanyi Intézet, 1961.

TCHINIANOV, A. : *Bratia Vesniny.* Moskva, Strojizdat, 1970. TEATRALNYE... *Teatralnye khoudojnik Rossii. Sbornik statej. «Tretia Khoudojestvennaia vystavka izobrazitelnogo iskousstva RSFSR».* Sovietskaia Rossiia, Khoudojnik RSFSR, 1970. THEATERARBEIT... *Theaterarbeit. 6 Aufführungen des Berliner Ensembles. Hrsg Berliner Ensemble, Helene Weigel.* Berlin, Henschelverlag, 1961 u. 1968. TIAJELYKH, V. : *N. V. Sitnikov.* Leningrad, Khoudojnik RSFSR, 1962. TRETIAKOV, N. : *G. Golts.* Moskva, Sovietskij khoudojnik, 1969.

VANSLOV, V. : *Izobrazitelnoe iskousstvo i mouzykalnyj teatr.* Moskva, Sovietskij khoudojnik, 1963. VANSLOV, V. : *Vadim Ryndin.* Moskva, Sovietskij khoudojnik, 1965. VANSLOV, V. : *Simon Virsaladze.* Moskva, Sovietskij khoudojnik, 1969. VIALE, Mercedes : *La scenografia del settecento e i fratelli Galliari.* Torino, F-lli Pozzo, 1963. VIALE, Mercedes : *Filippo Juvarra scenografo e architeto teatrale.* Torino, F-lli Pozzo, 1970. VIDETTA, Antonio : *Appunti per la storia della scenografia contemporanea.* Napoli, Libreria Scientifica Editrice, 1964. VIEFHAUS-MILDENBERGER, Marianne : *Film und Projektion auf der Bühne.* Emsdetten, Verlag Lechte, 1961. VLASSOVA, R. : *Konstantin Korovin. Tvortchestvo.* Leningrad, Khoudojnik RSFSR, 1970. VOLBACH, Walther Richard : *Problems of opera production, by Walther R. Volbach. Original drawings by John R. Rothgeb. Second rev. ed. s.l.,* Archon Books, 1967. VON EINEM, Gottfried und MELCHINGER, Siegfried : *Caspar Neher. Bühne und bildende Kunst im XX Jahrhundert.* Velber bei Hannover, Friedrich Verlag, 1966. VYSTAVKA... *Vystavka «50 let Sovietskoj teatralnoj dekoratsii».* Moskva, Sovietskij khoudojnik, 1971.

WARRE, Michael : *Designing and making stage scenery. Foreword by Peter Brook.* New York, Reinhold, 1966. WELKER, David Harold : *Theatrical set design, the basic techniques.* Boston, Allyn and Bacon, 1969. WILFRED, Thomas : *Projected scenery, a technical manual.* New York, Drama Book Shop, 1965 (Reprint). WOLFF, Hellmut Christian : *Oper. Szene und Darstellung von 1600 bis 1900. Musikgeschichte in Bildern, Bd IV : Musik der Neuzeit, Lieferung 1.* Leipzig, VEB Deutscher Verlag für Musik, 1969.

[YVES-BONNAT] : *Section Scénographique du Salon d'Automne 1971. (catalogue).*

ZIELSKE, Harald : *Handlungsort und Bühnenbild im 17. Jahrhundert.* München, Verlag Schön, 1965.

II. THE PLACE OF PRODUCTION

(Scenography in the wider sense, theatrical architecture, equipment, acoustics)

ACOUSTIQUE... *Acoustique et électroacoustique musicale. Facture instrumentale.* Paris, 1967. (Conférences des journées d'Etudes du IXe Festival international du son). ADAPTABLE... *Adaptable theatres : a report of the proceedings at the third Biennial Congress. Edited by Stephen Joseph...* London, ABTT, 1964. (Association internationale des techniciens de théâtre). ARCHITECTURE... *Architecture théâtrale.* (Documentation française - avril 1966 - nº 3282). ARKKITECHTILEHTI... Arkkitechtilehti 10-11/67. (magazin) [Helsinki], 1967. AUDITORIUMS... *Auditoriums and arenas : facts from a survey by the International Association of Auditorium Managers. Prepared under direction of the I.A.A.M. Publications Committee by Francis R. Deering, Don Jewell and Lindsley C. Lueddeke.* Chicago, Public Administration Service, 1961. (+ supplement, 1964).

BARANEK, Leo Leroy : *Music, acoustics and architecture.* New York, Wiley, 1962. BAUME, Michael : *The Sydney Opera House affair.* Melbourne-London, Nelson, 1967. BAZANOV, V. : *Stsena, tekhnika, spektakl.* Leningrad, Iskousstvo, 1963. BAZANOV, V. : *Teatralnaia tekhnika v obraznom reshenii spektaklia.* Moskva, Iskousstvo, 1970. BENTHAM, Frederick : *New Theatres in Britain.* London, Rank Strand Electric, 1970. BERGMAN, Gösta M. : *Den moderna teaterns genombrott 1890-1925.* Stockholm, Bonnier, 1966. BOWMAN, Ned A., COLEMAN, William and ENGEL, Glorianne : *Planning for the theatre.* Pittsburgh, University of Pittsburgh, 1965. BUDAPESTI... *A Budapesti Nemzeti Szinhaz tervpalyazata.* Budapest, Müszaki Könyvkiado Vallalat, 1966. BURMEISTER, Enno : *Möglichkeiten und Grenzen der Raumbühne.* München, Technische Hochschule, 1961. BURRIS-MEYER and COLE, Harold and Edward : *Theatres and auditoriums. Second edition.* New York, Reinhold Pub. Corp., 1964.

CANAC, François : *L'acoustique des théâtres antiques, ses enseignements.* Paris, Centre National de la Recherche Scientifique, 1967. COLLOQUIUM... *Colloquium über Theaterbau. Protokoll von der Deutschen Sektion des ITI, der Union Internationale des Architectes und dem Internationalen Music Council in Westberlin veranstalteten internationalen Tagung (21-25 November 60).* Berlin, Deutsche Sektion des ITI, 1961. CORRY, Percy : *Planning the stage.* London, Pitman, 1961. CRUCIANI, Fabrizio : *Il teatro del Campidoglio e le feste romane del 1513.* Milano, Il Polifilo, s.d.

DAY, Brian Frederick, FORD, R. D. and LORD, P. : *Building acoustics, edited by B. F. Day, R. D. Ford, and P. Lord.* Amsterdam-New York, Elsevier, 1969. DE'SOMMI, Leone : *Quattro dialoghi in materia di rappresentazioni sceniche.* Milano, Il Polifilo, 1968. DIVISIBLE... *Divisible auditoriums ; a report from Educational Facilities Laboratories.* New York, 1966. DUMONT, Gabriel P. : *Parallèle de plans des plus belles salles de spectacles d'Italie et de France.* New York, B. Blom, 1968 (Reprint).

FÊTES... *Les fêtes en Europe. Dix siècles de réjouissance. Choix de textes d'après l'ouvrage de H. BIEHN traduit par N. Montabetti enrichi de nouvelles pages françaises et de documents anciens recueillis par Simone Lamblin.* s.l., Club des Libraires de France, 1963. FRENZEL, Herbert A. : *Thüringische Schlosstheater. Beiträge zur Typologie des Spielortes vom 16. bis zum 19. Jahrhundert.* Westberlin, Selbstverlag der Gesellschaft für Theatergeschichte, 1963. FUNKE, Christoph, HOFFMANN-OSTWALD, Daniel und OTTO, Hans-Gerald : *Theaterbilanz 1945-1969. Eine Dokumentation über die Bühnen der Deutschen Demokratischen Republik.* Berlin, Henschelverlag, 1971.

GALLI da BIBIENA, Giuseppe : *Architectural and perspective designs dedicated to His Majesty Charles VI, Holy Roman Emperor, by Giuseppe Galli Bibiena. With an introd. by Hyatt Mayor.* New York, Dover Pub., 1964 (Reprint). GEERINCK, Marianne et Jacques : *Centres culturels. Réalisations architecturales.* Bruxelles, (Cahiers JEB - nos 2-3 mai 1965). GOOCH, D. B. : *Theatre and main street.* Ann Arbor, Printing Office of the University of Michigan, 1963. GRAUBNER, Gerhard : *Theaterbau Aufgabe und Planung. Mitarbeiter Frank D. Hemmer und andere.* München, Verlag Callwey, 1968.

HERZFELDT, Rudolf : *Deus ex Machina. La technique au service du théâtre.* Wiesbaden, Maschinenfabrik Wiesbaden GMBH, 1964. HIGH... *The high school auditorium : 6 designs for renewal : a report from Educational Facilities Laboratories.* New York, 1967. HINTZE, Joachim : *Das Raumproblem im modernen deutschen Drama und Theater.* Marburg, Elwert Verlag, 1969. HISTOIRE... *Histoire du lieu et du décor de théâtre. 90 diapositives. Commentaires d'Henriette Boulay et Lucienne Depraets.* Paris, Ligue de l'Enseignement, 1966. HOFFMANN, Hans-Christoph : *Die Theaterbauten von Fellner und Helmer.* München, Verlag Prestel, 1966. HÖGER, Gudrun e.a. : *Bühnentechnik - Beleuchtung - Requisit. Studienmaterial der Spezialschule für Leiter des künstlerischen Volksschaffens, Fachgebiet Laientheater.* Leipzig, Zentralhaus für Kulturarbeit, 1961 und 1965. HOLZBAUER, KURRENT und SPALT : *Der moderne Theaterbau und seine Entwicklung.* Wien, 1962. HUMMELEN, W. M. H. : *Inrichting en gebruik van het toneel in de Amsterdamse Schouwburg van 1637.* Amsterdam, Noord-Hollandsche Uitgeversmaatschappij, 1967. HÜTER, Karl-Heinz : *Henry van de Velde. Sein Werk bis zum Ende seiner Tatigkeit in Deutschland.* Berlin, Akademie-Verlag, 1967.

INGENIEUR... *Ingenieur - Taschenbuch Bauwesen. Band IV : Hochbau. Teil 2 : Entwurf. Herausgeber Prof. Heinrich Rettig.* Leipzig, B. G. Teubner Verlagsgesellschaft, 1966. IDEAL... *The ideal theater : eight concepts.* New York, American Federation of Arts, 1962.

JOB, Heinrich : *Theater für morgen.* Stuttgart, Karl Krämer Verlag, 1970. JONES, Eric : *Stage construction for school plays.* New Centre (Mass.), C.T. Branford Co., 1969. JOSEPH, Stephen : *Actor and architect.* Manchester, Manchester University Press, 1964. JOSEPH, Stephen : *New theatre forms.* New York, Theatre Arts Books, 1968. JOSEPH, Stephen : *Planning for new forms of theatre.* London, Strand Electric & Engineering Co 1962. JOSEPH, Stephen : *Theatre in the round.* London, Barrie & Rockliff, 196.

KINDERMANN, Heinz : *Bühne und Zuschauerraum, ihre Zueinanderordnung seit der Griechischen Antike.* Wien, Hermann Böhlaus, 1963. KRAUSE, Ernst : *Die grossen Opernbühnen Europas.* Berlin, Henschelverslag, 1966 u. 1968.

LAMORAL, R. : *Problèmes d'acoustique des salles et des studios. Préface de J.J. Matras.* Paris, Chiron, 1967. LIEU... *Le lieu théâtral à la Renaissance. Etudes réunies et présentées par Jean Jacquot.* Paris, Centre National de la Recherche Scientifique, 1964. LIEU... *Le lieu théâtral dans la société moderne. Études réunies et présentées par Jean Jacquot.* Paris, Centre National de la Recherche Scientifique, 1961. LIEUX... *Les lieux du spectacle - Osaka 70. Numéro conçu et réalisé par Christian Dupavillon.* Boulogne-sur-Seine (« L'Architecture d'aujourd'hui », nº 152 - octobre-novembre 1970). LOKALISERINGSUTREDNING... *Lokaliseringsutredning för ny Lyrisk teater i Göteborg.* Göteborg, 1966. LOUNSBURY, Warren C. : *Theatre backstage from A to Z.* Seattle, University of Washington Press, 1967.

Mc NAMARA, Brooks : *The American playhouse in the eighteenth century.* Cambridge (Mass.). Harvard University Press, 1969. MANKOUSKY, V.S. : *Acoustics of studios and auditorias.* New York, Hastings House Pub., 1970. MARCHI, Virgilio : *Note sulla scenografia. Vol. I : Propedeutica.* Roma, Centro sperimentale di cinematografia, s.d. MICHAEL, Wolfgang F. : *Frühformen der deutschen Bühne.* Westberlin, Selbstverlag der Gesellschaft für Theatergeschichte, 1963. MIELZINER, Jo : *The shapes of our theatre. Edited by C. Ray Smith.* New York, C. N. Potter (distributed by Crown Publishers), 1970. MILLER, James H. : *Self-supporting scenery.* Shreveport (Louisiana), E. T. Tobey Co., 1971. MULLIN, Donald D. : *The development of the playhouse ; a survey of theatre architecture from the Renaissance to the present.* Berkeley, University of California Press, 1970.

NEKHOROSHEV, Iou : *Khoudojnik i stsena.* Moskva, Iskousstvo, 1964. NEUTRA, Richard : *Gestaltete Umwelt. Erfahrungen und Forschungen eines Architekten. Hrsg. Hermann Exner. Mit 111 Abb.* Dresden, VEB Verlag der Kunst o. J., 1968. NIESSEN, Carl : *Theaterarchitektur contra Darsteller und Zuschauer - Eine Stachelschrift aus Gewissenszwang.* Köln, Institut für Theaterwissenschaft, 1960.

ODIN... *Odin Teatret. Théâtre - Laboratoire interscandinave pour l'art de l'acteur. Ornitofilene - Kaspariana - Ferai.* Holstebro (Danemark), Odin Theatrets Forlag, 1969.

POLIERI, Jacques : *Scénographie nouvelle.* Boulogne Seine, Editions d'Aujourd'hui, 1963. POLIERI, Jacques : *Scénographie. Sémiographie.* Paris, Denoël/Gonthier, 1971. PUPPI, Lionello : *Il Teatro Olimpico.* Vicenza, Neri Pozza, 1963.

QUIETZSCH, Heinz : *Die ästhetischen Anschauungen Gottfried Sempers. Mit 20 Abb.* Berlin, Akademie-Verlag, 1964.

RAES, A. C. : *Isolation sonore et acoustique architecturale. Problèmes techniques et solutions pratiques.* Paris, Chiron, 1964. ROBINSON, Horace : *Architecture for the educational theatre.* Eugene (Oregon), University of Oregon Books, 1970. RISSER, Arthur C. : *A theatre in a multi-purpose room.* Wichita (Kansas), 1962. RISSER, Arthur C. : *The educational theatre building and its equipment ; report of a study project conducted by Arthur C. Risser.* Wichita (Kansas), 1965.

SACHS, Edwin O. and WOODROW, Ernest A. E. : *Modern opera houses and theatres.* New York, B. Blom, 1968 (Reprint). SCHLEMMER, Oskar, MOHOLY-NAGY, Laszlo and MOLNAR, Farkas : *The Theater of the Bauhaus. Edited and with an introd. by Walter Gropius. Translated by Arthur S. Wensinger.* Middletown (Conn.), Wesleyan University Press, 1961. SCHMIDT, Diether : *Bauhaus. Mit Abb. und Grundissen.* Dresden, VEB Verlag der Kunst o. J., 1966. SCHÖPEL, Brigitte : *Naturtheater. Studien zum Theater unter freiem Himmel in Südwestdeuschland.* Tübingen, Tübinger Verein für Volkskunde, 1965. SCHUBERT, Hannelore : *Moderner Theaterbau. Internationale Situation. Dokumentation Projekte. Bühnentechnik.* Stuttgart, Karl Krämer Verlag, 1971. SILVERMAN, Maxwell and BOWMAN, Ned A. : *Contemporary theatre architecture ; an illustrated survey. A checklist of publications 1946-1964 by Ned A. Bowman.* New York, New York Public Library, 1965. SOSSOUNOV, N. : *Ot maketa k dekoratsii.* Moskva, Iskousstvo, 1962. SOUTHERN, Richard : *Proscenium and sight lines ; a complete system of scenery planning and a guide to the laying-out of stages for scene designers, stage-managers, theatre architects and engineers, theatrical history and research workers, and those concerned with the planning of stages for small halls. Rev. ed.* New York, Theatre Arts Books, 1965. SOUTHERN, Richard : *The Victorian theatre : a pictorial survey.* Theatre Arts Books, 1970. STAGE... *Stage planning. Fourth and fifth editions.* London, Strand Electric & Engineering Co., 1961-1962. STAHLKONSTRUKTION... *Stahlkonstruktion im Theaterbau.* Düsseldorf, Beratungsstelle für Stahlverwendung, 1961. STEREOPHONIE... *Stéréophonie et reproduction musicale.* Paris 1966. (Les cahiers de la Revue du Son, nº 7). SURVEY... *Survey of London. Vol. 35 : The Theatre Royal, Drury Lane and The Royal Opera House, Covent Garden.* London, Published for the G.L.C. by The Athlone Press, 1970. SWILLENS, P. T. A. : *Jacob van Campen, schilder en bouwmeester. 1595-1657.* Assen, Van Gorcum, 1961.

THEATRE... *Theatre architecture and stage machines. Engravings from the Encyclopédie, ou Dictionnaire raisonné des sciences, des arts, et des métiers. Edited by Denis Diderot and Jean le Rond d'Alembert.* New York, B. Blom, 1969 (Reprint). THEATRE... *Theatre check list : a guide to the planning and construction of proscenium and open stage theatres. Prepared by and published for the American Theatre Planning Board. With drawings by Ming Cho Lee.* Middletown (Conn.), Wesleyan University Press, 1969. THEATRE... *Theatre planning, reprinted from « The Architects' Journal ».* London, ABTT, 1964.

UNRUH, Walther : *Theatertechnik. Fachkunde und Vorschriftensammlung.*

Berlin, Klasing und Co, 1969. UNSERE...*Unsere Theaterneubauten nach 1945.* West-Berlin, Deutsche Sektion des Internationalen Theaterinstituts, 1967.

VALEIX, Danielle et BLOC, André : *Edifices culturels.* Boulogne-sur-Seine, 1967. (L'Architecture d'aujourd'hui, n° 129 - décembre 1966 - janvier 1967). VEINSTEIN, André : *Le théâtre expérimental.* Bruxelles, La Renaissance du Livre, 1968. VITRUVE : *Les dix livres d'architecture. Traduction intégrale de*

Claude Perrault. Paris, Balland, 1967.

WEBSTER, T. B. L. : *Griechische Bühnenaltertümer.* Göttingen, Vandenhoeck & Ruprecht, 1963. WEVER, Klaus : *Bauliche Forderungen des dialektischen Theaters.* (DISS). Dresden, 1965. WILLERS, U., SUNDSTRÖM, F. & MAR-KELIUS, . : *Stadsteater / City Theatre, Stockholm.* Stockholm, Fritzes hov-bokhandel, 1966.

III. STAGE COSTUMES

(to the exclusion of general works on costume)

BARTON, Lucy : *Historic costume for the stage.* Boston, Baker, Walter H., Co., 1961. BOULARD, Constance and DOUTEN, Hazel : *Costume drawing.* New York, Grosset & Dunlap, s.d. BROOKE, Iris : *Costume in Greek classic drama.* New York, Theatre Arts Books, 1962. BROOKE, Iris : *Western European costume and its relation to the theatre. Second edition.* New York, Theatre Arts Books, 1964. BROOKE, Iris : *Medieval theater costume ; a practical guide to the construction of garments.* New York, Theatre Arts Books, 1967.

CHINESE... *Chinese Opera Costumes.* New York, Orientalia Inc., 1967.

DOCUMENTS... *Documents pour le costume de théâtre. T. I à IV. T. I : Le Moyen Age. T. II : La Renaissance. T. III : Le XVIIe siècle. T. IV : Le XVIIIe siècle.* Paris, U.F.O.L.E.A., 1963-1967.

FERNALD, Mary : *Costume design and making : a practical handbook by Mary Fernald in collaboration with Eileen Shenton. Second edition.* New York, Theatre Arts Books, 1967.

JACKSON, Sheila : *Simple stage costumes.* New York, Watson-Guptill Pub., 1969.

KELLY, Francis Michael : *Shakespearian costume [by] F. M. Kelly. Completely rev. by Alan Mansfield. Second edition.* New York, Theatre Arts Books, 1970. KOMMISSARZHEVSKII, Fedor Federovich : *The costume of the theatre.* New York, Blom, 1968 (Reprint). KOSTIOUMY... *Kostioumy k tantsam narodov SSSR. Tsvetnye èskizy N. A. Lakova. Text i tcherteji kroia V. V. Sokolovskoj.* Moskva, Iskousstvo, 1964.

LAVER, James : *Costume in the theatre.* New York, Hill and Wang, 1965.

MOTLEY : *Designing and making stage costumes. American edition adapted by Susan E. Meyer.* New York, Watson-Guptill Publications, 1965. MOULTON, Bertha : *Garment - cutting and tailoring for students.* New York, Theatre Arts Books, 1968.

POOS, Eva : *Ruha a szinpadon.* Budapest, Népmüvelési Intézet, 1961. PRISK, Berneice : *Stage costume handbook.* New York, Harper & Row, 1966.

ROUSSKIJ... *Rousskij kostioum 1750-1917. Materialy dlia stsenitcheskikh postanovok rousskoj dramatourghii ot Fonvizina do Gorkogo. Albom v 5-ti vypouskakh. Ris. V. Kozlinskogo, text E. Berman i E. Kourbatovoj. Pod redaktsiej V. Ryndina, vypousk 3, 1850-1870.* Moskva, VTO, 1963.

SHARAFF, Irene : *Irene Sharaff Book on costume design.* New York, Van Nostrand Reinhold Co., s.d. SHAVER, Ruth M. : *Kabuki costume. Illus. by Soma Akira and Ota Gako.* Rutland (Vermont), C. E. Tuttle Co., 1966. SPENCER, Charles : *Erte.* London, Studio Vista, 1970. STAGE... *Stage costumes and accessories in the London Museum by M. R. Holmes.* London, HMSO, 1968.

TOMKINS, Julia : *Stage costumes and how to make them.* Boston, Plays inc. ; London, Pitman, 1969. TRÖSTER, Frantisek : *Costumes de théâtre. Introduction de Ludmila Vachtova.* Prague, Artia, 1962.

VOLLAND, Virginia : *Designing woman ; the art and practice of theatrical costume design.* Garden City (N.Y.), Doubleday, 1966.

ZAKHARJEVSKAIA, R. : *Kostioum dlia stseny.* Moskva, Sovietskaia Rossiia, 1967.

IV. LIGHTING

BELLMAN, Willard F. : *Lighting the stage : art and practice.* San Francisco, Chandler Pub. Co., 1967. BENTHAM, Frederick : *The art of stage lighting.* London, Pitman, 1970. BONGAR, Emmet W. : *Practical stage lighting.* New York, R. Rosen Press, 1971. BRONNIKOV, A. : *Osvetitelnoe oboroudovanie stseny.* Moskva, Iskousstvo, 1961.

COLOUR... *Colour filters for theatre lighting and other purposes [3944 : 1965] and Amendment PD 6059, March 1967.* London, British Standards Institution, 1965 and 1967. CORRY, Percy : *Lighting the stage ; with a foreword by Sir Tyrone Guthrie. Third edition.* London, Pitman, 1961.

FUCHS, Theodore : *Stage lighting.* New York, B. Blom, 1963 (Reprint).

HARTMANN, Louis : *Theatre lighting. Foreword by David Belasco.* New York, DBS Publications, 1970 (Reprint).

McCANDLESS, Stanley : *Syllabus of stage lighting. Eleventh ed.* New York, DBS Publications, 1964.

PEJL, V. : *Svet na stsene.* Moskva, VTO, 1966. PILBROW, Richard : *Stage lighting.* New York, Van Nostrand Reinhold Co., 1971.

SKRIABIN, A. : *Ekonomitchnaia portativnaia svetovaia apparatoura stseny. Opisanie skhemy konstrouktsii otdelnykh elementov i ouzlov i tekhnologhiia ikh izgotovleniia.* Moskva, VTO, 1964.

V. MAKE-UP AND MASKS

BARANSKI, Matthew : *Mask making. Revised ed.* Worcester (Mass.), Davis Publications, 1966. BERNOLLES, J. : *Permanence de la parure et du masque africains.* Paris, Maisonneuve et Larose, 1966. BOUBIK, Vlastimil : *Art of make-up for stage, television and films.* Elmsford (N.Y.), Pergamon Press Inc., 1968.

CORSON, Richard : *Stage makeup. Fourth ed.* New York, Appleton-Century-Crofts, 1967.

HALL, Heinz : *Maskenspiel und Schminke. Einige Erfahrungen über die Herstellung, die Anwendung und das Spiel von einfachen Masken und über das Schminken.* Leipzig, VEB Friedrich Hofmeister, 1961. HUNT, Kari and CARLSON, Bernice Wells : *Masks and mask makers.* New York, Abington, 1961.

KEHOE, Vincent J. : *The technique of film and television make-up for color and black and white. Second rev. ed.* London-New York, Focal P., 1969.

LISZT, Rudolph G. : *The last word in make-up, illustrated by the author. Rev. ed.* New York, Dramatists Play Service, 1963. LU, Steve : *Face painting in Chinese opera.* New York, DBS Publications, 1969.

MALYGHINA I., D. SITNOV i L. SNEJNITSKIJ : *Grim i kostioum v sovremennom spektakle.* Moskva, Iskousstvo, 1963. MELVILL, Harald : *Magic of make-up, by the most modern methods for stage and screen, with drawings by the author.* New York, Theatre Arts Books, 1969.

PEROTTET, Philippe : *Practical stage make-up.* New York, Reinhold Pub. Corp., 1967.

TERRY, Ellen and ANDERSON, Lynne : *Make-up and masks.* New York, Rosen, Richards Press Inc., 1971.

VAGO, Zsofia : *Jelmez és környezettörténet II - III.* Budapest, Népmüvelési Intézet 1959-1960.

INDEX OF ILLUSTRATIONS LISTED UNDER DESIGNERS

INDEX OF ILLUSTRATIONS LISTED UNDER PLAYWRIGHTS AND COMPOSERS

This index is in two parts :

The first part contains spoken plays listed under authors. Plays which have no playwright are listed under the group's name. The second part contains music theatre works (operas, musical comedies, ballets...) listed under composers.

I

PLAYWRIGHTS

Playwright	Original title and translation in English	Designer	Illustr.
TOLSTOJ, Alexej	Smert Ivana Groznogo *The Death of Ivan the Terrible*	Soumbatashvili, Iossif	230
TRIANA, José	La Noche de los Asesinos *The Assassins*	Egemar, Christian	384
TRIANA, José	La Noche de los Asesinos *The Assassins*	Eichbauer, Helio	383
TRIANA, José	La Noche de los Asesinos *The Assassins*	Gubbels, Klaas	385-386
TSURUYA, Nanboku - SUZUKI, Tadashi	Natsushibai, Howaito komedii *Summer Play, White Comedy*	Takada, Ichirô	185

V

Playwright	Original title and translation in English	Designer	Illustr.
VALLE-INCLAN, Ramon Maria del	La Marquesa Rosalinda *Marquise Rosalinda*	Nieva, Francisco	216
VAN ITALLIE, Jean-Claude	America Hurrah	Leontov, Tania	409
VON KLEIST, Heinrich	Penthesilea	Oechslin, Ary	187

W

Playwright	Original title and translation in English	Designer	Illustr.
WALCOTT, Derek	The Dream on Monkey Mountain	Burbridge, Edward	378
WEISS, Peter	Die Ermittlung *The Investigation*	Palmstierna-Weiss, Gunilla	332
WEISS, Peter	Die Ermittlung *The Investigation*	Schmückle, Hans-Ulrich	333
WEISS, Peter	Gesang vom lusitanischen Popanz *The Song of the Lusitanian Bogeyman*	Ahmed, Samir	340
WEISS, Peter	Gesang vom lusitanischen Popanz *The Song of the Lusitanian Bogeyman*	Keserü, Ilona	548
WEISS, Peter	Gesang vom lusitanischen Popanz *The Song of the Lusitanian Bogeyman*	Mau, Waltraut - Träbing, Ilse - Weiffenbach, Klaus	338
WEISS, Peter	Gesang vom lusitanischen Popanz *The Song of the Lusitanian Bogeyman*	Palmstierna-Weiss, Gunilla	339
WEISS, Peter	Die Verfolgung und Ermordung Jean Paul Marats, dargestellt durch die Schauspielgruppe des Hospizes zu Charenton, unter Anleitung des Herrn de Sade *Marat - Sade*	Egemar, Christian	337
WEISS, Peter	Die Verfolgung und Ermordung Jean Paul Marats, dargestellt durch die Schauspielgruppe des Hospizes zu Charenton, unter Anleitung des Herrn de Sade *Marat - Sade*	Nieva, Francisco	545

Playwright	Original title and translation in English	Designer	Illustr.
WEISS, Peter	Die Verfolgung und Ermordung Jean Paul Marats, dargestellt durch die Schauspielgruppe des Hospizes zu Charenton, unter Anleitung des Herrn de Sade *Marat - Sade*	Palmstierna-Weiss, Gunilla	335-336
WEISS, Peter	Die Verfolgung und Ermordung Jean Paul Marats, dargestellt durch die Schauspielgruppe des Hospizes zu Charenton, unter Anleitung des Herrn de Sade *Marat - Sade*	Weiss, Peter	334
WEISS, Peter	Vietnam Diskurs *Vietnam Discourse*	Asakura, Setsu	343
WEISS, Peter	Vietnam Diskurs *Vietnam Discourse*	Palmstierna-Weiss, Gunilla	341-342
WILLIAMS, Tennessee	Camino Real	Wexler, Peter	323
WITKIEWICZ, Stanislaw Ignacy	Bezimienne Dzielo *The Anonymous Work*	Kolodziej, Marian	237
WITKIEWICZ, Stanislaw Ignacy	Kurka Wodna *The Water Hen*	Kantor, Tadeusz	232-233
WITKIEWICZ, Stanislaw Ignacy	Matka *The Mother*	Kolodziej, Marian	238
WITKIEWICZ, Stanislaw Ignacy	Wariat i Zakonnica *The Madman and the Nun*	Kantor, Tadeusz	234-236
WYSPIANSKI, Stanislaw - GROTOWSKI, Jerzy	Akropolis *Acropolis*	Szajna, Jozef - Grotowski, Jerzy	223-224

Y

Playwright	Original title and translation in English	Designer	Illustr.
YOU BEIJING WEN HUA GONG ZUOZHE, GONG REN, NONG MIN, XUE SHENG JITI BIAN	Dong Fang Hong *The Red Orient*	You Beijing Wen Hua Gong Zuozhe, Gong Ren, Nong Min, Xue Sheng Jiti Bian	426

Z

Playwright	Original title and translation in English	Designer	Illustr.
ZETTERHOLM, Tore	Kvinnorna fran Shanghai *Women from Shangai*	Egemar, Christian	324
ZHONGGUO WUJUTUAN JITI GAIBIAN	Hong se ninang zi jun *The Red Women's Detachment*	Zhongguo Wujutuan Jiti Gaibian	427

II

COMPOSERS

Composer	Original title and translation in English	Designer	Illustr.

B

Composer	Original title and translation in English	Designer	Illustr.
BARTOK, Béla	A Csodalatos Mandarin *The Miraculous Mandarin*	Daydé, Bernard	462
BEETHOVEN	Fidelio	Lees, Allan	431
BEJART, Maurice	Baudelaire	Bernard, Roger - Roustan, Joëlle	522
BEJART, Maurice - HENRY, Pierre	Nijinsky, Clown de Dieu *Nijinsky, Clown of God*	Bernard, Roger - Roustan, Joëlle	550-551
BERG, Alban	Wozzeck	Mulas, Ugo - Puecher, Virginio - Colciaghi, Ebe	467-469
BERG, Alban	Lulu	Vernet, Thierry	470-472
BERIO, Luciano	Allez - Hop !	Luzzati, Emanuele	519
BERLIOZ, Hector	Les Troyens *The Trojans*	Georgiadis, Nicholas	438-439
BIZET, Georges	Carmen	Gregotti, Vittorio - Fioroni, Giosetta	449
BIZET, Georges	Carmen	Sokolova, Marina	450
BIZET, Georges	Carmen	Messerer, Boris	451

Composer	Original title and translation in English	Designer	Illustr.
BLACHER, Boris	Zwischenfälle bei einer Notlandung *Incidents during a Forced Landing*	Bill, Max	487
BRITTEN, Benjamin - PURCELL, Henry - HOLST, Imogen	Dido and Aeneas	Vossen, Frans	494
BRUBEK, Dave	Jazz-out	Yves-Bonnat	539

D

Composer	Original title and translation in English	Designer	Illustr.
DALLAPICCOLA, Luigi	Ulisse *Ulysses*	Wendel, Heinrich	488-489
DESSAU, Paul	Herr Puntila und sein Knecht Matti *Squire Puntila and his Servant Matti*	Reinhardt, Andreas	476-479

CONTENTS

ILLUSTRATIONS